Reckless Courage

Reckless
COURAGE

The True Story of a Norwegian Boy Under Nazi Rule

WILLIAM F. FULLER

WITH JACK HAINES

The Taber Hall Press   Marion, Massachusetts

First published in the United States of America in 2005
by Taber Hall Press.

For information about permission to reproduce sections
from this book, write to Taber Hall Press, P.O. Box 159,
Marion, Massachusetts, 02738.

ISBN 0-9769252-0-6

Book Design by Sonia Shannon
Edited by Abigail A. Fuller

Printed in Canada by Transcontinental Printing

Cover: King Haakon VII's emblem painted on walls was
a widespread symbol of protest.

The cover photograph appeared without attribution or
copyright in Norway and the Second World War, a 1966 paper-
back published by Johan Grundt Tanum Forlag, an Oslo
firm no longer in existence. Aschehoug, the firm that
purchased the Tokens of Norway Series, of which this is a part,
does not have archives that go back that far. They would have
granted permission to use the photograph if their ownership
was clear but suggested we use it and note our effort
to identify the copyright holder.

Third Softcover Printing

To the Norwegians
A Magnificent Peace-Loving And Compassionate People

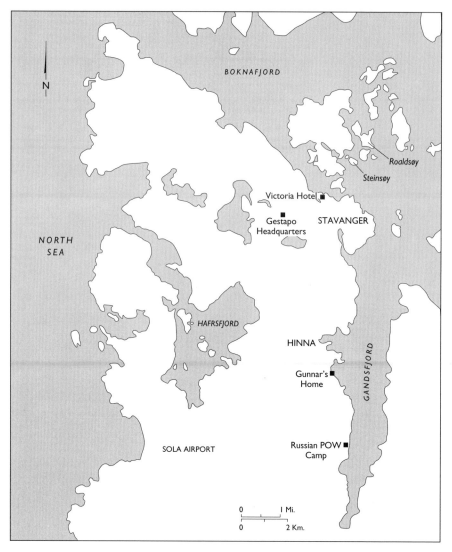

Stavanger and Surroundings

Contents

Norway and Northern Europe, April 1940

Preface

The skeleton-like figures surrounding him in the darkness could not understand how this thirteen-year-old Norwegian boy had been able to get into the prison camp—or why he would risk his life to bring them a little food and tobacco.

hile I was recuperating from surgery, visiting nurse Susan Haines Mechler told me about her father's reaction as a boy in Norway during World War II when he witnessed starved Russian prisoners snatching up bits of horse manure to eat. I asked her to record and write down more about her father's expereiences. Gunnar Haines (originally Høynes, in the Norwegian) was terminally ill at the time, and after his death I helped Susan put together a memorial booklet about his life and experiences during the occupation. While working on it, I became intrigued with the importance of Norway in World War II and how little recognition by historians this has received. A good case can be made that Hitler's decision to invade Norway cost Germany the war and changed the course of history. I believe it did, and my reasons are outlined in the appendix.

I could not bear to leave out descriptions of several of the most glorious naval actions in British history as well as some tragic comic aspects of Norway's defense. Nowhere have I come across the idea that Norway's monopoly on "heavy water" production adversely impacted German efforts to build an atomic bomb. I believe it was significant, and my thoughts on this are spelled out in an appendix following military and naval anecdotes. I have also included a brief history of this unique nation and a description of the Viking Age and the ships that roamed the seas from North America to Baghdad.

The main story is, of course, about the experiences of a Norwegian family during the occupation and how their teenage son became a thorn in the sides of the Germans. Gunnar Haines left a legacy of courage and compassion. By including historical aspects of the occupation with interesting anecdotes, I hope this book will spread that legacy beyond a currently small circle of family and friends.

William F. Fuller
Marion, Massachusetts
August 2004

Acknowledgements

y greatest debt is to Gunnar's older brother, Jack Haines (Jakob Høynes). He provided most of the details about the family during World War II and without him the book would not have been possible, nor as pleasant a project. Gunnar's daughter, Sue Mechler, who first told me about her father's exploits, and Anna Vigre, Gunnar's sister, who showed me sites in the Stavanger region, both deserve special recognition and my thanks. I am also indebted to Norwegians I interviewed about their recollections of the occupation years. They are Sigrid and Gunnar Gundersen, John Isaksen, Gudrun Birkeland, Berger Nøst, Nils Roaldsøy, Knute Aarsheim, Tor Arneberg, Martin Enoksen, Professor Reidar Dittmann of St. Olaf College, and Eivind and Sylvia Strand. Finally, I must include Wenche Lund of the *Stavanger Aftenblad* newspaper and Per Meldahl for permission to use the photograph by Henry Meldahl of Jakob with the resistance group at war's end.

While I was conducting research in Norway, Steffen and Maryan Tunge, Arne and Torhild Enoksen, and Arild and Anne-Karin Tvedt could not have been more hospitable and were such delightful company. Rolf Hodne, manager of the Victoria Hotel that is so prominent in the story, and Hans Storhaug, author of a book about the hotel and head of the Norwegian Emigration Center, were both too generous with their gifts and guidance.

My family and friends helped in so many ways, and I thank them, particularly my wife, Barbara, and my cousins, Hugh Rawson and Margaret Miner, authors and editors, for holding my hand throughout; Gayle Haines for comments and advice; my daughter, Abigail Fuller, for editing; Sonia Shannon of the Yale University Press for her wonderful design and help with publishing; and Beth Walker of Walker & Co., a longtime friend who encouraged me to write the book.

Chronology Of Norway During World War II

1939

September 1	Germany invades Poland, World War II begins.
November 30	Russia invades Finland.
December 14	Quisling meets Hitler and makes up story about secret British deal with Norway and Carl Hambro, the Jewish President of Parliament.
December 17	German raider *Graf Spee* scuttled at Montevideo, Uruguay.

1940

February 16	British destroyer frees prisoners from the *Altmark* in a Norwegian fjord.
February 19	Hitler orders Norway invasion.
March 13	Finland surrenders to Russia.
March 20	British postpone invasion of Norway.
April 8	British mine Norwegian coastal waters south of Narvik.
April 9	German invasion officially begins at 4:15 a.m. (Norwegian time). At 7:30 a.m. King Haakon with ministers and gold reserves escape from Oslo. Quisling announces NS Party takeover on radio at 7:30 p.m.
April 10	Local radio station broadcasts King Haakon's call to resist.
April 10 and 13	Naval battles at Narvik, ten German destroyers

	lost plus supply ships.
April 14	Start of British and French landings in north at Namsos.
May 7 and 8	Historic British Parliament debates centered on Norway campaign.
May 10	Winston Churchill replaces Neville Chamberlain as British prime minister.
May 27-June 4	335,000 Allied troops trapped at Dunkirk, France are evacuated to England.
June 7	King Haakon and the government leave Norway for England.
June 10	Italy enters the war against France.
June 21	Formal surrender of France.
September 25	Norwegian Constitution abolished by Reichskommissar Terboven.

1941

March 4	Commando raid on Lofoton Islands by 450 British and 52 Norwegian Resistance fighters from Linge Company.
March 27	Hitler orders destruction of Belgrade, begins Balkan campaign.
June 22	Germany invades Russia. Jews in northern Norway interned.
August	Start of radio confiscation in Norway, except for military and Quislings.
December 27	British Commando raid at Vaagso and diversion raid in Lofoton Islands.
December 29	Hitler orders troop reinforcements and capital ships from France to Norway.

1942

January	24 "court hostages" interned, including Odd Nansen, head of relief organization.
February 1	Quisling appointed "Minister President."
February	Teachers ordered to join "New Front" under NS Party control.
February-March	Alesund and Televaag executions and reprisals for Norwegian resistance.
March-April	Teachers reject new union; 1,300 imprisoned and 700 brutalized.
August 3	King's birthday, 283 arrested in Oslo for carrying flowers.
October	Death penalty instituted for radio listening or possessing anti-German literature.
October-November	Jewish men, then women and children, arrested.
December-February	760 Jews sent to Auschwitz; a handful survive.
December	German 6th Army (nearly 300,000 troops) surrounded at Stalingrad.

1943

February	German surrender at Stalingrad; psychological turning point of the war.
February 28	Sabotage of Norsk-Hydro "heavy water" production.
July 10	Allies invade Sicily.
August	Internment of 1,175 former Norwegian Army officers.
September	German battleship *Tirpitz* put out of action in fjord anchorage but stays afloat.

November 30	1,200 Norwegian students arrested, 700 imprisoned in Germany; Himmler outraged by damage to planned SS recruiting effort.

1944

February 20	"Heavy water" equipment and last supply from Norsk-Hydro destroyed.
June 6	D-Day; Allied troops land at Normandy.
September	Finland surrenders to Russia; Germans retreat to Norway.
October-November	Finnmark (northern section of Norway) devastated by scorched earth policy.
Winter 1944-1945	Harshest winter of the war; severe food shortages.

1945

April 30	Hitler commits suicide in Berlin bunker.
May 7	General Boehme broadcasts German surrender of Norway at 10:15 p.m..
May 8	Church bells celebrate throughout the land at 3:00 p.m. for a full hour.
June 7	King Haakon returns to Oslo, five years to the day after leaving Norway.

Prologue

With law shall we build our land, not with

lawlessness lay it waste.

Introduction to Norway's ancient code of laws

Norway has a wild mystic quality and a spectacular beauty that is unlike any other place in the world. Its 1,600-mile coast has 150,000 islands and is heavily indented with fjords. One even extends 125 miles inland, contributing to the approximately 20,000 miles of water frontage. Sheer, towering cliffs border the fjords and small farms hang precariously along the water's edge. Distant snow-capped mountains reach as high as 8,000 feet. Seventy-five percent of the land is mountainous and only four percent is arable. Most soil is quite shallow and easily leached out. Even before the Viking era in the eighth century, the land could not adequately support the population. Until recently, there has been continual emigration. The difficulty of working small infertile farms in isolated settlements and relying on one of the world's most treacherous seas to survive has forged a hardy and independent people.

Although the blood of Vikings flowed in their veins, at the start of World War II the overwhelming majority of the three million Norwegians were fervently committed to peace. Norway had remained staunchly neutral in World War I, was one of the strongest supporters of the League of Nations, and her humanitarian work, particularly in saving children following the ravages of that war, received worldwide acclaim. Norwegians could not imagine any nation violating their neutrality. Although Germany's admirals did want bases in Norway for direct access to the North Atlantic, Hitler was more interested in Norway remaining neutral so Swedish iron ore could be shipped down its coast without interference from Britain. Besides, they felt Britain's ten times larger navy was prepared to block any German attempt to invade. Norwegians were concerned when Germany invaded Poland in September 1939 but felt more threatened when Communist Russia declared war on neighboring Finland three months later. How wrong they were.

In the predawn hours of April 9, 1940, Nazi Germany invaded neutral Norway with two parachute battalions, over eight hundred aircraft, ten thousand advance troops from three divisions, and virtually the entire German navy. Just before nine o'clock, nine-year-old Gunnar Høynes and his older brother Ingolf were on their way to school outside Stavanger when German bombers roared overhead. The planes, their black crosses outlined in white, were so low that faces could be seen in the gun turrets. The boys were frightened and started to run.

By noon the Germans had seized all key targets: eight coastal cities; Oslo, the capitol; and the Stavanger and Oslo airports. It was one of the most audacious, quick, and brilliantly executed operations in World War II. British forces already embarked to invade the northern coast of Norway in an attempt to cut off Germany's iron ore from Sweden were completely taken by surprise, as were the Norwegians.

In Berlin that evening an exuberant Hitler congratulated himself on a stunning victory. It probably cost him World War II and his dream of a "Thousand Year Reich."

1

NORWAY, DECEMBER 1939

Mor, gi'mig solen. (Mother, give me the sun.)

Henrik Ibsen, *Ghosts*

It was still dark that December morning when Mathilde Høynes slowly climbed the stairs to the third floor attic to wake the three boys. Jakob, sixteen, slept in a room of his own, while Ingolf, twelve, and Gunnar, nine, shared a room at the other end. On school days she tried to get the boys up and moving as soon as the bathroom on the second floor was free. Marion, fourteen, and Ivar, the father, were already in the dining room, dressed and having breakfast. Laid out on the white tablecloth was a pitcher of milk, a platter of thick slabs of homemade light brown Norwegian bread, and side dishes of butter, cheese, and sardines. Marion was up early to help her mother with one-year-old Anna, while Ivar had to leave early to catch the bus for downtown Stavanger. He handled all blending in the city's largest margarine plant, one of many enterprises founded by a great uncle. It was an important job, insuring that the margarine was neither too liquid nor too hard despite changes in seasonal temperatures.

Mathilde switched on the overhead light in the wide hall between two bedrooms before going around to gently shake each boy's shoulder and telling them it was time to get up. An erect, taller than average woman, she shuffled through the rooms in slippers and an apron tied at the waist that she always wore indoors. She took clean plaid wool shirts out of the large hall dresser for each of the boys before pulling off the down comforters to air out the beds. Gunnar, of slight build and serious manner, was invariably the first one dressed and down to wash. Ingolf and Jakob were usually arguing over whose turn it was to feed Rex, the family's pet Boxer. Ingolf, stocky and well built but a head shorter than his lanky older brother, was a constant tease in trying to get a rise out of Jakob but was generally unsuccessful. Jakob had more serious things on his mind that morning.

Three weeks earlier, the Russians had invaded Finland. A volunteer force from Sweden and Norway was being formed to aid the small neighboring country that was battling giant Russia to a standstill in the winter forests. The day before, while visiting a friend's house after school, Jakob had overheard an older brother pleading with his parents to let him join. The father was unusually emotional in arguing against it. His main point was Norway's long tradition of pacifism and neutrality, aside from the fact it was bound to be a losing cause. His friend's mother said nothing, and his brother listened silently with his head hung. Norwegians did not argue with their parents. Although Jakob was two years too young to enlist, he could not get the idea of joining this noble cause out of his mind.

Gunnar sat down for breakfast dressed in a heavy hand-knit

wool sweater, thick corduroy knickers, knee-length black wool stockings, and winter boots. He said good morning to his father, who was about to take a cup of coffee into the study to catch a few minutes of Radio Norway's seven o'clock news. Ivar wanted to hear the latest developments in Finland before catching the bus. Everyone at the plant was talking about the war. Finland bordered Norway in the far north section of the country, and most Norwegians feared Communism and Bolshevik Russia as much as Nazi Germany.

Gunnar bolted down his breakfast so he could join his father in the study for a few minutes. Ivar, who the children called Far, was lean, clean-shaven, and slightly balding with a placid, kindly face. He sat in his favorite easy chair while Gunnar crouched next to him. After the major news items, Ivar looked at his wristwatch and stood up. He had to leave to catch the bus but told Gunnar to stay and listen. There were too many important world events the boys should know about. Ivar got his overcoat and Hamburg hat from the front closet, touched Mathilda on the cheek, patted the three children, and headed down the front walkway to the main road. Gunnar watched from the study window until his father was beyond the giant fir trees and out of sight.

Mathilde sent Gunnar back up to the third floor to hurry Jakob and Ingolf along. She spent the next hour making sure everyone had a full breakfast and was ready for the school day. Anna watched from the high chair as her older brothers and sister told Mor what type of open faced sandwich they wanted for lunch. They had a choice of either sliced egg or sardine, which Mathilde wrapped in waxed paper. She made a last minute check of Gunnar's and Ingolf's leather school satchels to make sure each had the right notebooks for that day's classes. All Norway followed the same schedule.

The Høynes Home in Hinna

After seeing the children off, Mathilde put Anna on her lap and had her first cup of coffee and a few minutes rest. Rex, wagging his tail and still not fed, stood expectantly at her knee. She decided that starting tomorrow, she would turn that chore over to Gunnar. Ingolf was always getting sidetracked and had to be constantly reminded, while Jakob should be doing more grown up tasks. It was now nine o'clock, but the sky was just getting bright and the sun still had not risen above the mountains across the fjord. Still, the six hours of sunlight this time of year seemed like a blessing. Mathilde thought of a girlhood friend who had married and moved to the northernmost city of Hammerfest. There, the sun completely disappeared for two months from late November until late January. There was only a glow in the sky for several hours at mid-day.

Mathilde had a full schedule and wanted to finish her Christmas shopping in Stavanger before the children returned from school. She was also expecting a delivery truck around noon with a surprise for Ivar and the family. The entire month of December was taken up with the typical Norwegian preparations for Christmas: every piece of metal polished, all linens and clothes washed and ironed, woodwork and walls scrubbed. Dried cod, thin and as hard as a wooden board, had to be soaked for days in a lye solution and then pounded with a mallet to make *lutefisk,* the traditional national dish for the occasion. Although the children helped after school and on the weekends, Mathilde still carried the extra workload of caring for Anna and keeping house. Because of the cool climate, like most Norwegians Mathilde did not have an icebox or refrigerator, and so in addition she had to make almost daily trips into the center of Hinna for milk and other perishables.

Mathilde

Mathilde did not regret buying the large home in the Hinna suburb, but it required far more work than the rental in Stavanger from which they had moved three years ago. The three-story gray house with brown trim sat on a large plot of land overlooking the Gandsfjord, a narrow spur of the very wide Boknafjord that extended out to the North Sea twenty miles to the west. There was a garden in back and several tall fir trees in front. The house was on the main road to Stavanger, across from a communal dock where they kept their twenty-foot double-ended skiff. Behind the house, low hills provided some protection from the prevailing and often violent west winds off the North Sea. December days were often calm, with just a dusting of snow on the ground, like this morning when Ingolf and Gunnar made the twenty-minute walk to school. Situated on the west coast in the southern part of Norway, Stavanger was only 280 miles from the Scottish Isles and like them had surprisingly mild weather due to the continuation of the Gulf Stream, called the North Atlantic Drift. Average winter temperatures were just above freezing, but further inland there were arctic conditions and mountains heavily clad with snow.

SCHOOL AND HOME

The world is only saved by the breath

of the school children.

The Talmud

unnar and Ingolf arrived at the white two-story elementary school in Hinna just before the nine o'clock bell. Gunnar's fourth grade class had Mr. Opsal, who taught the same twenty-odd students through all seven years of elementary school. Mr. Opsal was elderly and had been Jakob's teacher as well. In fact, he had just finished with Jakob's class before starting Gunnar's four years ago. Nearly all the teachers in Norway were men and it was one of the most respected professions. Once everyone was settled at their desks, Mr. Opsal began by formally welcoming the children and asking them to open their books to a prayer. Religion was traditionally the first subject, and after the prayer they sang a hymn.

Although Norway was the only European nation with an official state religion, the Lutheran instruction in schools was low key and not overemphasized. Gunnar and the others enjoyed singing the hymns, and the prayer or lesson was always brief before they started other subjects. The fourth graders learned math, history, geography, Norwegian, drawing, and nature studies. Everyone expected to be called on by Mr. Opsal at least once during the day to recite or answer some question. As they stood by their desks, students were graded on elocution, politeness, and posture. Politeness was particularly emphasized in Norwegian education and Gunnar always received high marks in this regard. This quality, combined with his innocent appearance and calmness under pressure, would later help save his life.

Between class subjects, the students were given ten-minute breaks, just enough time to race outside, get fresh air, and have a few words with friends. At noon, there was a half-hour recess for lunch, and if the weather was good, students had ten or fifteen minutes to kick a soccer ball around in the small field next to the school. The school had no organized sports or extracurricular activities and both Gunnar and Ingolf, could hardly wait to be Jakob's age and join the local soccer club. Until then, there were pick up games, ice skating at an outdoor pond, and skiing for a few of the children whose parents took them twenty miles or so inland to the mountains on weekends and holidays. Finally, at two o'clock the bell rang and Gunnar grabbed his coat and satchel to catch up with Ingolf and the older boys heading home. The sun, very low on the horizon, had already disappeared behind the hills west of Hinna and would set in less than an hour.

When the boys got home, Mor was all excited, with an unusual sparkle in her eyes. She helped them off with their coats, and with a finger to her lips whispered, "I have a Christmas surprise for Far.

Ivar, Rex, and Gunnar at War's End

Come." When she opened the door to the formal living room used for visitors, Gunnar hardly recognized it with all the new furniture: two easy chairs, a divan, a round table for the tea service, new lamp shades, and a bright blue rug with gold floral designs. He recalled only the two large bookcases and some small side tables from before. Mor had not changed the wallpaper, though. Gunnar remembered his father's joke that the house didn't need studs to hold up the walls considering the number of layers of paper they had pasted on. Mor did not expect much reaction from the boys, but she was very pleased with the change and could hardly wait for Marion and Jakob to arrive by bus from Stavanger and, of course, Ivar from work. Changing the décor and replacing the furniture was one of her joys in life. She would eagerly look through magazines on the store rack for pictures of the royal family's rooms to get new ideas for the house.

When Marion and Jakob came home an hour later, they exclaimed how fine everything looked. The real excitement, however, was Far's arrival and his performance. "Tilda, my princess. Am I in the right house?" he asked as he turned about, making sure to show surprise and wonderment. He wanted to please her and make the children laugh, and he succeeded. They all adored him, particularly Gunnar, who had developed a special relationship with his father last summer when a prank backfired.

Gunnar had found some firecrackers and decided to try an experiment. He extracted a tablespoon of powder and packed it tightly down in the hollow tube of a closet key. Then he rigged up a firing mechanism with a sharp nail, a cap gun cap, and a long string. When he jerked the string, the nail hit the cap, triggering a shattering blast. When the smoke cleared, Gunnar could not believe what had happened. There were wood splinters all over the floor and a charred, gaping hole where the closet knob had been. The acrid smell of burnt gunpowder was everywhere. In a panic, he ran down the stairs and out the back door to the neighbor's barn, where he climbed up in the loft to hide. After what seemed like hours, he heard the screen door of his kitchen bang shut. A few moments later, he heard his father at the barn entrance calling in a soft voice, "Gunnar! Are you all right?" "Ja, Far," came his choked reply. Ivar said, "Please come down then." When Gunnar did, Ivar took him by the hand back to the house and did not mention the incident again. Gunnar never forgot.

3

CHRISTMAS IN HINNA

It is good to be children sometimes, and never

better than at Christmas when its mighty Founder

was a child Himself.

Charles Dickens

hristmas Eve was especially exciting for Gunnar this year. For weeks, he had been hinting to his mother about a present he hoped to get. He would find out that evening. By noon, Marion and Mathilde had set out the dried cod, now a soft and flakey *lutefisk*. It was served with boiled potatoes and butter, dried green peas cooked to a mush, ruta- bagas, and sliced pork. The best part for Gunnar was the vast array of at least seven different kinds of cookies and cakes that were passed around later in the living room during coffee. Some of the adults and visiting relatives enjoyed a light snooze while Gunnar showed his visiting five-year-old cousin, Nils, his room upstairs and some of his treasures.

Before long it was time to get ready for church and the five o'clock Children's Service. Although the Høyneses were a God-fearing family, they were not active churchgoers except on special occasions like baptism, confirmations, weddings, funerals, and a few Holy Days. Nevertheless, Gunnar and his brothers and sister had all attended Sunday school regularly at the Bede Hus in Hinna, a small, special chapel-like structure designed for this purpose that was just beyond the elementary school. Today everyone donned their best clothes and boarded the bus for the Hetland Church, the Høynes family's church and gravesite on the hill above Stavanger's Old Town. Ivar led the way up from the bus stop toward the tall white steeple while the bells rang forth in staccato-like bursts, a special style of ringing for this holiday. The minister kept the service short, as he knew the children were on pins and needles waiting to get back to their homes.

Back home, Ivar disappeared behind the closed door of the living room for ten minutes or so, then emerged and gathered everybody in the hall. With a flourish, he opened the door. There stood a dazzling Christmas tree lit with white candles, and in a corner dozens of wrapped presents. Everyone joined hands around the tree, and after a short prayer by Ivar, they slowly circled while singing hymns, carols, and folk songs. Gunnar could not concentrate as he tried to spot his name on the presents. At last the singing ended, and at a signal from Ivar, the children scrambled to find their gifts. Anna got a doll; Marion, an embroidered party dress; Ingolf, boxing gloves and shorts; and Jakob, a ski jacket. Gunnar gasped at his shiny new socket wrench set, pliers, and a screwdriver set. From an early age, he had been fascinated with engines and how they worked. It was exactly what he had hoped for. He relished the smell of the light coating of preservative oil.

Ivar tapped his spoon against a water glass to get everyone's attention. He reminded the children that Christmas was a celebration of the birth of Christ, that gifts and presents were secondary, and that there was much to be thankful for, especially this year. Although war was breaking out all over Europe and in neighboring Finland, Norway was still at peace. Norwegians were much better off than just several years ago when unemployment was over 30 percent and cod sold for a penny a pound. Finally, looking at the children he said, "We sure better not forget to take care of the *nisse*. We don't want those troublemaking elves with red stocking caps to get mad at us if we don't give them some of our best food."

Mathilde had already prepared a plate along with a bundled sheath of wheat to tack outside for the birds. There was also a tradition of special treats for animals, and Rex qualified. Gunnar asked if he could take care of these chores, as Ingolf and Jakob were already starting to tangle and Marion was showing Anna how to play with the new doll. He set the *nisse's* dish out on the back porch and hung the sheaf of wheat on a nail in the post by the door. He put Rex's dish down in the pantry, away from the *nisse's* food, and hurried back to the dining room. At last, the family and guests sat down around the table for a light meal of porridge followed by individual bowls of rice pudding. Expectation built as they waited to see who would get the one with the almond, and in a few minutes Marion gave an uncharacteristic whoop of joy. She was a quiet and somewhat shy girl and for her to get the prize was especially pleasing to everyone. Marion unwrapped and generously shared pieces of the prize, a marzipan pig.

That night Gunnar took his new tools to bed with him, but he had trouble getting to sleep thinking about what he could start to work on and whether Jakob would make him a wooden tote box. His efforts to sleep were not helped by Ingolf dancing around in his new boxing outfit, trying to goad Jakob into a few rounds.

Long before dawn, Gunnar was awake and in the basement with his new tools, cleaning off the sticky preservative coating with kerosene and thinking about the job he really wanted to tackle someday: the Model T Ford boat engine. He had watched Far and Jakob tinker with the recalcitrant machine, and last summer for the first time he felt confident of taking it apart to find out what was causing it to conk out at unexpectedly awkward moments. It had done this several times when crossing the busy ship channel on Sunday visits to his grandparents' Steinsøy Island farm. Gunnar was still wondering how best to approach his father with the idea when he was called up for breakfast, a special treat of thin, heart-shaped waffles.

All day the family would be receiving visitors and going to see relatives and friends, so Ivar took Jakob and Ingolf aside for a private talk about behaving. More pleading than demanding, Ivar asked them not to tease or fight this special day. These talks did not always work, and Ivar was not a disciplinarian. Out of love and respect for this gentle man, the children did try, but there were embarrassments. In fact, some of Mathilde's friends, when asking her to visit, had begun saying, "Perhaps you could just bring Gunnar." In any case Jakob now had more on his mind than jousting with his brother. He was discovering that several of the girls he had known for years but not thought much about now caught his attention. He also noticed more than a few darting glances from them.

One relative who created unusual excitement for everyone was

Ivar's cousin, a doctor with the same name, who drove out from Stavanger in his new Renault car. He took everyone for a short ride and spent time showing Gunnar all the workings of the engine. Dr. Høynes was quite distinguished, having recently been appointed head of the Stavanger school system's health department. He had received his medical training in France and was the Høynes family doctor, but he refused to ever send a bill.

After the holidays, when the children were back in school, Mathilde joined a group of women friends to knit woolens for the Finnish army and the volunteer regiment from Norway and Sweden. Norwegians felt a special closeness with the Finns, who they saw as hardy like themselves, not soft and effete like the Danes and Swedes. Most in demand were white knit items such as scarves, caps with earflaps, and mittens with a slit for the trigger finger. In the movie theaters, the hearts of the world were captured by newsreel shots of white clad Finns suddenly appearing on skis out of the snow-laden forests to pick off Russians, and as quickly melting back into the landscape. The more than ten-to-one numerical superiority of the Russians, however, was gradually taking its toll. By mid-February 1940 it appeared that the Finns could not hold out much longer. Ivar heard rumors that Britain and France had approached the Norwegian government for permission to land troops in Norway and go across on a rescue mission. It was inconceivable to Ivar and his friends that the country would agree and risk becoming the battleground in a war between England and Russia, with Germany sure to join in.

Ivar became more concerned on February 17 when he heard on the evening news that during the night a British destroyer had entered neutral Norwegian waters just south of Stavanger. In the Jossingfjord, a boarding party had reportedly freed hundreds of British seamen prisoners from the German ship *Altmark*. Norway's foreign minister protested strongly to the British government, but this failed to satisfy Germany. Hitler was furious that two Norwegian gunboats had stood by and watched without putting up a fight. A month later, things got worse. Finland surrendered, and the number of Norwegian merchant ships torpedoed by German submarines kept increasing. Of course, Germany always reported these as accidental. Norwegians felt threatened after the *Altmark* incident but counted on the British navy to intervene if Germany got too aggressive. In fact, the government even felt it was safe to send half its small 13,000-man army way north for maneuvers against a potential Russian threat. Hopes to avoid a conflict diminished quickly, however, when a shocked nation heard on the April 8 evening news that Britain had laid mines along the Norwegian coast to stop ships carrying Swedish iron ore from the port of Narvik to Germany.

4

THE INVASION

The bravest operation in German war history.

Hitler

When Gunnar and Ingolf left for school on Tuesday morning, April 9, 1940 the sky was crystal clear, after several days of gale force winds had swept in from the North Sea. They were halfway there when they first became aware of the far-off drone of airplane engines. The sound grew louder with each step, and suddenly there was an ear-shattering roar as bombers shot right over their heads. Dozens of them passed at such a low altitude that Gunnar could make out faces in the gun turrets. The noise was deafening, and he was scared. Much higher in the sky, smaller planes with black crosses outlined in white on their wings circled around. The two boys were only a few hundred yards from school, and they ran as fast as they could. A teacher stood out front telling the arriving students to return home immediately. He tried to appear calm, assuring the children that everything was going to be all right, but Gunnar and Ingolf knew something momentous was happening. They ran most of the way home, sprinting faster whenever there was an explosive boom in the distance.

Jakob had already finished his private school term in Stavanger. Early that morning, he went out to climb one of the taller hills about two miles west of the house. While enjoying the smells of the awakening spring and the clear morning sky, he too heard the increasingly loud drone of airplanes, and looking west was startled to see a low-flying twin engine bomber heading straight for his hill. It swerved as though aiming at him, and Jakob threw himself on the ground just as it swooped up and over. His first thought was that it was Finnish because of the crosses on the wings, but like his younger brothers, he headed home as fast as he could.

Mathilde was standing outside waiting when Ingolf and Gunnar ran up to the front stoop. Next to her stood a neighbor who had been listening to Radio Norway at 8:30 a.m. when Foreign Minister Koht, in a surprise broadcast, announced that Germany was invading the country and the armed forces were being mobilized. Without thinking, he added that King Haakon and the government had left Oslo an hour earlier for Hamar and Elverum, sixty miles north. The Germans were delighted to hear this, since they had been searching desperately to find and capture the king and government ministers.

Mathilde now realized the planes were German, but she learned little else as Radio Norway soon shut down and was off the air most of the day. She hustled the children and Rex indoors as more German planes zoomed overhead. Jakob arrived a few minutes later, and then they started to worry about Marion and Ivar in Stavanger.

When Ivar got off the bus that morning, he had a feeling something unusual was going on. There were far more cargo ships at anchor than he had ever seen, and one of the workmen he met going into the factory said there were several large shiploads of horses in the harbor. Fishermen returning home near dawn had heard whinnies and snorts from these ships. An hour into the workday, Ivar's manager yelled from the door of his office that Oslo radio was reporting a German invasion, and that the armed forces were being mobilized. Work stopped and everyone gathered around, wondering what was happening. Then they heard the airplanes. Ivar and others went out onto the street overlooking the harbor just in time to see squadrons of low-flying bombers coming in over the water. High above, fighter planes circled along with Stuka dive bombers. The Stukas dove with high-pitched sirens proclaiming their lethal descent. It was like the newsreels Ivar had seen of Germany's devastating assault against Poland seven months earlier. The few bombs dropped were meant to frighten people, and just about everyone quickly retreated indoors.

Ivar could not get a phone line to call Mathilde, but soon the manager decided to send everyone home except a skeleton staff. After covering up the mixing line and changing out of his white coveralls, Ivar left the factory just in time to see a squad of Germans at the end of the street marching past. They wore long gray-green coats with rifles slung on their shoulders and distinctive German army steel helmets. The sidewalks were full of people, mostly men, staring in stunned silence. Looking over at the wharf, Ivar saw one of the large cargo ships tied up, with giant German flatland horses (the first of sixteen thousand) being led down boarding ramps. Back toward the city center, he saw the blood–red German flags with their black swastikas already flying over some municipal buildings. It almost broke his heart.

With a population of forty-seven thousand, Stavanger was

Norway's fourth largest city and the major sardine canning center. Most of the innovations in processing and vacuum packing for the industry came from here as well. It was Norway's principal location for quality printing, a side product of making can labels. Stavanger was also an important emigration port and shipbuilding area. The flatlands along the coast south of Stavanger were very fertile and the region was often referred to as the nation's breadbasket. However, all of these factors were secondary to Germany's main interest: Sola Airport. Just a few miles southwest of the city, it was not only Norway's largest airport but one of Germany's most strategically important targets and a key to the invasion's success. From Sola, the Germans could control the air along most of the coast, as well as the entrance to the Baltic Sea between Denmark and Norway. The planes that Gunnar and his brothers saw that April morning were part of an armada that flew up from Germany and Denmark. The formation stayed out at sea, flying only a few hundred feet in altitude to avoid detection, before turning toward land opposite Stavanger. Eleven planes dropped 130 parachute troops on Sola Airport. The parachutists quickly overcame the one machine gun section that put up any defense, and by day's end nearly one hundred JU-52 transport planes brought in 2,000 more troops. They commandeered trucks and cars and entered Stavanger without opposition.

Ivar took a back street over to the main bus terminal, but nothing was running and a large crowd was milling about. When he learned that the Germans had already seized most of the buses and it was impossible to get a taxi, he decided to start walking. It was then about eleven o'clock. The main road south out of Stavanger to Hinna and inland was jammed with all sorts of vehicles, horse–drawn carts, bicycles, and pedestrians. There was an eerie quiet except for the airplanes. Hardly anyone spoke, even though movement was at a crawl because the Germans had set up roadblocks. When Ivar reached the barrier, he was waved through quickly. He proudly flashed his driver's license; not many Norwegians had them, and Ivar was quite peeved that the sentry did not even want to look at it. The soldiers were primarily interested in weapons and men of military age, and Ivar, with his black felt hat and fairly new overcoat, looked more like a banker. He practically trotted the last mile and almost cried with relief when he saw Mathilde and the boys out front anxiously waiting for him. Marion, who was inside with Anna, had only reached home an hour earlier. Teachers at her school had divided the students into groups and accompanied them to their homes around the city. Mathilde had the teakettle going and shepherded everyone into the dining room for a hastily prepared snack. Hardly a word was said, but there were frequent glances out the window at vehicles and people streaming by.

Ivar tried the radio in the study. Radio Norway was silent. He was finally able to tune in Radio Stockholm. Germany was reporting an overwhelming victory, announcing that all major cities and targets had been taken and that a planned British and French invasion had been foiled. Germany also announced the complete surrender of Denmark by the king and government. London's BBC (British Broadcasting Corporation) was reporting major British naval engagements and successful air strikes. Stockholm had no news of Norway's king and government, only that they had left Oslo before the Germans arrived. It did report, however, that sporadic Norwegian army resistance was developing. Later in the afternoon, Ivar and neighbors gathered outside the house to talk things over. No one had a clear idea what was going on, or what they were supposed to be doing. The main subject was the swift German takeover and how it could have happened. Where were the Norwegian armed forces? It would be weeks before many of the details and events would be known.

That evening, shocked Norwegians heard a surprise broadcast at 7:30 p.m. over Radio Norway, now back in operation under German control. Vidkun Quisling, whose name would become synonymous with traitor, had bullied his way into the Oslo studio and grabbed the microphone. He announced that Germany had come to protect Norway from the British and that his Nasjonal Samling (Norwegian National Unity, or NS) party was taking control, since the government had abandoned its responsibilities by leaving Oslo. This was a surprise to the Germans, as Quisling's small four-thousand-member fascist party had little credibility among the people. When Hitler's ambassador called him for instructions, Hitler asked, "Why not Quisling?" But Quisling lasted only six days before he was pushed aside. The damage, however, had been done. His emergence as the proposed leader of the nation repelled most Norwegians and was the key factor in King Haakon's refusal to agree to any terms with Germany. Ivar and his friends could not believe what they were hearing. They were particularly concerned by Quisling's closing threat that any resistance would be severely punished.

No one slept well that night. In the morning, Mathilde decided that Marion should stay home for a few days until the situation in Stavanger was clarified, but Ivar headed off in the darkness to see if he could get a bus ride into town. Mathilde and the boys, watching from the door, saw no buses operating, and she worried that there might be trouble in Stavanger. A few hours later, German fighter planes engaged in aerial combat with British bombers. The British were sending over waves of bombers in an attempt to disable Sola Airport, now a heavy concentration of Luftwaffe aircraft. After several ships were sunk in the harbor and a few British bombs landed in Hinna, some of the Høyneses' neighbors started to panic. There were rumors that the entire Stavanger area would be leveled by bombs, and they talked of abandoning their homes to join relatives in the countryside. Hearing this, Mathilde, wondered if she and the children should consider leaving. Which would be safer: her family's farm on the island of Steinsøy just offshore from Stavanger, or Ivar's parents' home in Skudenes, twenty miles away at the entrance to the North Sea?

5

A TURBULENT DAY

After the first confusion peaceful Norway had to be

conquered in hard fighting to the utter amazement

of the Germans....

—Halvdan Koht and Sigmund Skard, *The Voice of Norway*

Ivar set out for work the next day, thinking about the bombing and wondering what, if anything, the family should do. One section of the basement was partitioned and would be a good shelter from air raids, and perhaps it would be best for the family to wait and see what happened. He passed the roadblock easily and was not surprised to still see more traffic heading out of the city than going in. Downtown, soldiers appeared to be patrolling everywhere in twos and threes or passing by in trucks, automobiles, and horse-drawn wagons. The few civilians about stood morosely watching in silence.

Most of Ivar's associates showed up on time, but little work took place. They gathered in small groups to ask questions and exchange stories. Their muted conversations were interspersed with anxious glances toward the windows and doors. Though there was not a German in sight, there was little doubt they would show up. Within the hour, their presence was felt when the manager called Ivar into the office. He had just received a call from the Victoria Hotel seeking an extra delivery of margarine. The Germans had taken over the hotel for use by their higher-ranking officers, and the hotel staff was frantically calling around for extra food and supplies.

Just a few blocks away, the five-story red brick Victoria Hotel overlooked the passenger steamer docks. Built in 1900, it was without question Stavanger's largest and finest hotel with seventy rooms and a staff of twenty-five. Ivar was a friend of the assistant manager and volunteered to deliver extra tubs of margarine himself. He was curious to hear what was happening. He shed the white coveralls and put on his suit jacket before leaving. At the hotel, Ivar stayed almost an hour, sitting in a quiet corner of the kitchen where he listened and sipped coffee while his friend and other employees recounted the previous day's events. Around ten o'clock in the morning, a German captain had appeared in the lobby and asked to see the manager. He was impeccably dressed, with a monocle, light gray gloves, knee-high polished riding boots, wide flared trousers, and a belt with a pistol holster and sheathed dagger. He was the perfect Hollywood image of a Prussian-bred officer.

The hotel's housekeeper, who happened to be a British sympathizer, quickly appeared. She explained that Mr. Axel Lund, the owner-manager, was not expected for another hour or so, but could she help? The officer politely informed her that the hotel would be taken over for use by the German forces. All occupants were to be out and the rooms cleared by early afternoon. The housekeeper promised to alert the staff and start the process, but asked the officer to come back in a couple of hours when Mr. Lund was expected. In fact, she was stalling for time. Clerks from the British Consulate office on the street behind the hotel were burning documents and code books in the hotel's large basement boiler that very minute. To further complicate matters, the Consul General, along with several of his staff and a wireless operator, was in a second floor reception room anxiously watching the harbor. He was half expecting the British navy to arrive any minute. Downstairs, the German visitor acknowledged the housekeeper's request with a courtly bow, clicked his heels, and left, much to the relief of the onlooking staff.

The housekeeper raced downstairs to hurry up the burning and round up some work clothes for two uniformed British military attaches who were still trying to contact Britain on their wireless radio. There was a loud explosion in the street outside. A small bomb blew out glass in several windows and a piece of the balcony on the second floor fell to the street. No one was sure whether it was an accident or the beginning of an air raid. The housekeeper frantically urged the British to clear out as fast as possible. Soon the small party was assembled at the back entrance and crammed into a waiting taxi.

A few hours later Mr. Lund arrived. He and his wife Ellen lived at another hotel he owned, the Sola Strand, which overlooked a long sandy beach on the North Sea eight miles away. All morning, roads in the area had been closed off after parachute troops had secured Sola Airport. They then took over the Sola Strand. Mr. Lund was not in a happy mood when he finally arrived in his chauffeur-driven car that narrowly escaped seizure by the Germans. Born in Denmark, the forty-seven-year-old Lund was an impressive, aristocratic looking man, always well dressed with stiff white collars and a bowler hat. He usually carried a gold knobbed cane and a beautifully embroidered carpetbag briefcase. His early training had been at the world famous Adlon Hotel in Berlin. Later he had acquired a small chain of hotels in Denmark and Norway. He bought the bankrupt Victoria in the early 1920s and completely turned its fortunes around. Lund and the Victoria Hotel would have a major influence on Gunnar Høynes's life in a few years.

Lund listened to the housekeeper's report and agreed they had no choice but to comply and make the best of the situation. He called the department heads into his office down the long hall behind the reception desk and, every inch in command, instructed them to calmly go about their duties and live up to the Victoria's reputation as the best run and most sophisticated hotel in southwest Norway. While bewildered and angry guests milled around the lobby and crowded the reception desk demanding attention, another German officer with an armed enlisted man entered and asked to see the manager. He introduced himself as Dr. Gobel. Lund, looking down his nose at the rumpled uniform and quite unmilitary appearance of this officer who looked more like an accountant, replied, "If you're Dr. Goebbels" (the German propaganda minister but with a different spelling),"I am Mussolini" (Italy's dictator). The German saw no humor in this, but the exchange spread like wildfire among the hotel's staff and was like a tonic. Ivar finished his coffee, thanked everyone, and left by the delivery entrance. He could hardly wait to pass on the gossip.

Rather than return by the harbor road, Ivar walked up the hill behind the hotel through the narrow back streets where most of the shops were located. He was startled to see German soldiers pouring out of the stores loaded with bundles, and he stopped an onlooker to ask what was going on. Apparently Germany's years of preparation for war had not encompassed luxury goods and decent clothing. Even poor Norway's shops had much better quality and more to offer. The Germans were on a buying spree, paying with IOUs for inflated bank notes soon to follow. The looting of Norway had begun.

The Germans had already arrived at the margarine plant by the time Ivar returned. Three of them were in the manager's office: an officer with a notebook who was jotting down answers to questions, and two enlisted men carrying rifles. With typical German efficiency, they wanted to know all the key details of the operation. They were quite impressed to learn that with eighty employees, the plant was one of the largest in Norway. Ivar and the other employees went through the motions of working, glancing frequently towards the office. Concerned about his family, Ivar would have been even more upset to know that Gunnar and several school friends were only a few blocks away.

Gunnar's school had been let out early following a brief run-through of the class work. The children were told that Stavanger school buildings were being taken over by the Germans and to let their parents know this probably would happen in Hinna as well. The teachers again urged everyone not to worry or be afraid. They reassured the children that they would try to keep classes going; fortunately, the term was almost completed. But instead of going home, Gunnar and a few friends went into Stavanger. They were not expected home for several more hours and could not contain their curiosity. By noon their little group was standing on a downtown sidewalk watching soldiers march by. The gray-green uniformed troops looked very pleased with themselves, and most waved and smiled at the wide-eyed Norwegian youngsters. Little did they realize that the most innocent looking one with brown eyes and light brown hair would become such a thorn in their sides.

A few days later, Jakob and a friend were also downtown watching the activity. They were looking in a bakery window when a German soldier came alongside. He pointed, and in halting and barely intelligible Norwegian asked an elderly man standing beside them what the donuts on display were called. Peter and Jakob did a "double take" at the answer. The elderly Norwegian walked rapidly away, but the boys could not help going inside to see what would happen. At the counter, the soldier asked the wide eyed proprietor for "two assholes, please." The boys had to turn their backs. By late evening, a sizeable number of friends and relatives enjoyed the story.

STEINSØY ISLAND

Oh, it's a snug little island!

A right little, tight little island.

Thomas Dibdin

For the remainder of the week, Mathilde worried about her parents. Ivar decided that the family ought to visit them Saturday when he got home from work. They would then forego their traditional Sunday visit and instead take the two-hour ferry ride to Skudenes to check on Ivar's relatives. Mikal and Anna Steinsøy, Gunnar's grandparents, lived and farmed on a small island five miles north of Hinna and within rowing distance of downtown Stavanger. The house and barns stood on a flat section at the north end of the island, and rocky cliffs rose on both sides to a promontory nearly a hundred feet high at the southern point. The island resembled a horseshoe, with an enclosed tree-lined pasture in the valley that inclined up toward the summit. It was a typical small Norwegian farm with chickens, goats,

The Steinsøy Farmhouse

a pig, and two cows. There was electricity but no interior plumbing; sponge baths were taken discreetly in a corner of the kitchen. The rustic reminder of life in the past was enchanting to the youngsters, and it was an idyllic place during harvest time when many relatives came to help.

On Steinsøy, Mathilde would take the boys out before breakfast to check the fishing lines they had baited and set out the night before. They almost always pulled up a good catch of cod and an occasional eel. After ample quantities of fresh milk, brown goat cheese, and slabs of home baked bread, the grandparents assigned chores. This was Mikal's domain and he gloried in his commanding role. The men and older boys mowed the hay with long-handled scythes while the younger boys and girls raked and stacked. The men, spaced ten feet apart, rhythmically cut in rows for most of the morning, stopping only to sharpen the blades with whetstones and gulp down water spiked with a little oatmeal and salt to prevent cramps in very hot weather. When the stacks grew tall enough, Gunnar, when little, would climb up a ladder and leap down onto the soft lower piles. His younger cousins now followed suit. Anna, Mathilde, and the other women cleaned and filleted the fish catch, cleared the breakfast table, washed utensils, and prepared the picnic lunches. The summer picnics would be one of Gunnar's fondest memories during the winter days ahead.

After work stopped for the day, usually around two o'clock, blankets and tablecloths were spread on the grass for a sumptuous feast of homemade bread and cakes, herring or fresh cod, *syltetøy* (Norwegian waffles with fresh jam), and coffee. The older boys usually sat together and chatted in an old steam launch tied to the dock, while the littlest children raced around playing games. The youngest were not the only ones who played, however. One afternoon last summer, Ingolf had stripped down in the woods up in the valley for a game of cowboys and Indians. He pasted on chicken feathers to make a loincloth and headdress, and with hatchet raised, the Steinsøy Indian burst out of the bushes on his unsuspecting siblings. Unfortunately, his bounding leap and a strong gust of wind blew away most of the feathers, nearly revealing more than his sister and a girlfriend cared to see. That summer the three boys had built a giant bonfire at the highest point of the island on Midsummer's Eve, June 23, and from across the ship channel it could be seen by almost all of Stavanger. It was to be their last bonfire for another five years.

Ivar and Mathilde decided to take their motorboat for the forty-minute trip to Steinsøy, since much of the bus service to Stavanger was suspended and ferry service to the nearby islands was uncertain. Ivar guessed that petrol would soon be scarce, but he was afraid this might be one of the few times they could use the boat to bring supplies back from the farm. Gunnar always tried to go along for the chance to work the choke and throttle on the Model T Ford engine while his father hand cranked it to start. Also, he had a deal with his father to take over the helm for part of the trip. Now that one of Gunnar's chores was feeding Rex, he had a constant tail-wagging companion around home and got permission to bring Rex along. German patrol boats came close but no one stopped them. Rex rode in the bow, his front paws up on the gunwale and his muzzle defiantly thrust forward. Gunnar laughed when Far said that the Germans were probably scared off by this ferocious monster emulating the prow of a Viking warship—although it might have been Ivar's habit of loudly singing hymns while at the helm that kept them at bay. The real reason Rex stayed forward was the jolt he got last summer from inquisitively nosing the spark plug.

Ivar cut the engine and easily coasted the last few yards to the dock where Mikal and Anna were waiting. Mikal, in his early seventies, had unusually perceptive hearing. Almost five minutes earlier he had recognized the familiar sound of the engine just as he always heard someone whistling from the adjacent island of Hundvag signaling him to row across and pick them up after the ferry ride from Stavanger. Mathilde and Ivar spent a few hours there to be sure everything was all right. Yes, a German launch with soldiers had pulled up to their dock that morning and an officer had poked around and asked questions about the farm. The German duly made note of the livestock and facilities and even looked into the *stabbur,* the shed raised four feet on stilts where a two-year supply of food stocks was traditionally stored. He also reported that the army was taking over the small island just a stone's throw north with three large oil storage tanks and a small farmhouse. The German was polite and assured them that life would go on as before. Mikal did not seem in the least worried, but Ivar teased his father-in-law by feigning concern. "Far, I hope you didn't tell them about your stay in America." Mikal had spent several years there in the late 1880s and always made a point of telling new acquaintances and even reminding old friends, "When I was in America..."

They loaded the boat for the trip home with several sacks of manure, potatoes for planting, and vegetable seedlings Anna had started in a cold frame. Everyone knew there would be food shortages. Ivar loved to dig and grow things in the backyard and although Mathilde liked fishing more than gardening, she enthusiastically pitched in. After docking at Hinna and putting things away in the pantry, Mathilde relieved Marion and got Anna ready for bed. On his way up to the attic with a book, Gunnar stopped and listened for a few moments outside Anna's bedroom. Mor was softly singing his favorite nursery songs. "A, var jeg en sangfugl" ("Oh, If I Were a Songbird") and "I Am Little But I Will Always Belong to Jesus." After Anna was asleep, the rest of the family gathered in the dining room. Marion knitted. Jakob whittled a spar for a ship model. Ingolf and Gunnar read while Ivar and Mathilde played a simple card game. When Mathilde had a poor hand, she invariably sighed and gave it away with, "My cards are so bad." Like most Norwegians, she was guileless and lacked cunning.

7

THE DISMAL MONTH OF MAY

The worst is not, so long as we can say,

"this is the worst."

Shakespeare, *King Lear*

unnar left early Sunday morning from Stavanger with his father and Marion for the two-hour ferry ride to Skudenes on the Island of Karmøy. His grandparents, Jakob and Gurina, had a farm less than a mile west of the harbor. They were eagerly waiting. They had rounded up as many relatives as possible for a reunion Sunday dinner, including Gundersen cousins who lived in northern Karmøy near the French-owned mines that supplied copper for America's Statue of Liberty. Gunnar Gundersen was engaged to Sigrid Larsen and years later they would live just a few miles from Gunnar Haines in Massachuetts. Jakob looked like a Biblical Prophet with his trimmed white beard that went from ear to ear. He quizzed Ivar on events in Stavanger but had to admit he had seen little of the Germans other than air combat overhead. After dinner, Gunnar and Marion went with their father to call on the Isaksens, parents of Ivar's boyhood friend, Josef, who had emigrated to America seventeen years earlier. Although they stayed in touch and wrote frequently, Ivar was surprised to find the Isaksens' daughter-in-law, Janna, and her two-year-old son John. She was visiting her family further down the coast and was very concerned about getting home to Brooklyn where she and Josef had settled. In fact, it would take her five years, including over six months in the Grini concentration camp near Oslo, before she would see her husband again.

The last two weeks of April 1940 were a blur as Germany poured more troops and supplies into the country and Norwegians had little news about the war or military operations. As the nation recovered from a state of shock, talk spread that there must have been a traitorous conspiracy for the Germans to so easily take over the country. Norwegians who understood English listened to the BBC while others tuned in to Sweden's Radio Stockholm. German-controlled Radio Norway only issued a steady stream of propaganda about German military victories. The Germans constantly reminded Norwegians that they had come to Norway's defense against a British and French invasion, and they were soon dubbed "the Salvation Army." The regular German troops were unusually well behaved, and the dreaded Gestapo police and their fanatical SS military brothers had scarcely made their appearance. Norwegians were just now hearing of the dramatic sinking of the *Bluecher,* with its thousand men and Gestapo records in the Oslofjord, which had given the king and government time to escape.

When school ended in May, Gunnar's days settled into a routine of chores after breakfast for an hour or so before joining friends for a pickup soccer game, stopping to watch aerial combats or German units go by, or sharing stories about the occupation. In the afternoons, he usually ran errands for his mother and picked up the mail at the postmistress's home in the village center. Then he waited for his father. Now that bus service had been severely curtailed, Ivar did not get home until near five o'clock. Gunnar continued to listen to the news with him after supper, and until the middle of the month, Ivar had some hope the small Norwegian army along with the British and French in the far north might turn things around. Then beginning on May 10, in a matter of days it seemed as though the world was turning upside down.

> *Little holiday steamers made an excursion to hell*
> *and came back glorious.*
> Winston Churchill, speaking of the rescue of 335,000
> Allied troops trapped at Dunkirk

On May 10, Neville Chamberlain, Britain's Prime Minister, resigned due to British failures in Norway. On the same day, the German army started its blitzkrieg sweep through France and in two weeks conquered Belgium and Holland and encircled an entire British army at Dunkirk on the coast of France. More meaningful to Gunnar was the Germans' cancellation of the May 17 Constitution Day parade that celebrated Norway's most important holiday. He and his friends had been looking forward to the morning children's parade through downtown Stavanger, with everyone waving Norwegian flags. They usually bought lunch from a street vendor while waiting for the afternoon parades of clubs, organizations, and graduating students. Now only small groups could assemble. In place of the parade, Ivar decided to pull out the Norwegian history books and refresh his memory of the 1814 Constitution. He planned to go over it with the family after supper. Although the story of how the Constitution evolved was covered in school, Gunnar and the others were on the edge of their seats hearing Far retell it so movingly in this tragic period.

Norway had been part of Denmark for over three hundred years, until 1814 when it was given to Sweden because Denmark had been on the losing side in the Napoleonic wars. Left alone during the war, Norwegians tasted independence for six years and were not about to accept domination by Sweden. In 1814, Norwegians called a constitutional assembly in the small town of Eidsvoll, some forty miles up country from Oslo. There, 112 delegates from all walks of life met for almost six weeks without a break, eating together and lodging in adjacent farms. Some even shared beds. They thoroughly studied and discussed other constitutions and political philosophy tracts before settling on something close to the U.S. Constitution of 1787. They even read French translations of several of the original thirteen state's constitutions printed especially for the French by Benjamin Franklin. After the signing on May 17, a short war with Sweden ensued before a compromise was worked out giving Sweden control of foreign affairs but leaving Norwegians otherwise independent. All noble privileges and titles were abolished and Norway finally had a true democracy. Only the United States supported Norway against Sweden and the Great Powers—Great Britain, Russia, and Austria. Ivar related this history very solemnly until near the end when he talked of America's backing. He knew that since this beacon of liberty was not yet committed in the war, there was still hope. Pointing this out made for an upbeat finish and the entire family felt a lot better. Gunnar felt his first stirrings of wanting to see and know more of this land that Janna Isaksen and Far had talked about in Skudenes.

One of Gunnar's greatest thrills in the first weeks after the invasion was joining Jakob after dark to watch the distant flashes of gunfire from British warships. From a hill about a fifteen minute climb west of the house they had an unobstructed view of Sola Airport and the North Sea beyond. Reddish orange bursts of light on the horizon were followed by a long delay before Jakob and Gunnar would hear the explosion of the shells landing around the airfield. Eight years earlier, the British battleship HMS *Rodney* had made a courtesy visit to Stavanger and Ivar had taken the boys aboard. The British sailors had made a fuss over little two-year-old Gunnar, and Jakob wondered if by chance that same ship was over the night horizon. (It was!) Keeping Sola in operation was critical for control of the air along the southern half of Norway's coastline and any damage was quickly repaired by the following morning. If there was aerial combat during the day, Gunnar and his friends would climb the hill for a better view. They were enthralled when a German plane went down in flames trailing smoke or splashed into the sea. Often a parachute followed. It was a new and exciting time for the children, but not for the adults who were beginning to experience the heel of German occupation with all its rules and brutal punishments.

8

GERMANY TIGHTENS
THE SCREWS

Close your hearts to pity! Act brutally! The stronger

man is right. Be harsh and remorseless. Be steeled

against all signs of compassion!

Hitler to his generals, August 22, 1939

With France being overrun and Britain virtually defenseless, the Allies pulled out of Norway on June 8, 1940, leaving Germany in complete control. Many Norwegians felt betrayed and Gunnar could see the pain on his parents' faces when they heard King Haakon's departing speech the next day on the radio. Although the nation's gold reserves and merchant marine had been kept from Germany, Ivar questioned the effectiveness of the new government in exile. It seemed Hitler had all he wanted and no one was able to challenge him. Ivar wondered what was in store for poor Norway, which unlike Denmark had refused an "accommodation" with Germany and put up a fight.

Within days of the invasion the Germans imposed blackout restrictions to foil British nighttime bombing attempts. They requisitioned trucks and municipal buildings and took surveys of farms and businesses. Soon almost every facet of life was being regulated with German efficiency. It was not long before the Gestapo's secret police selected an isolated building on the fringes of downtown Stavanger for their headquarters and torture rooms. German administrative personnel were also soon overseeing all state and municipal functions. Historically in warfare the vanquished had been treated better by the follow-up civil administrators than by victorious soldiers who raped and pillaged. The Nazis reversed this pattern. Most of the Nazi party members and leaders sent into Poland and other conquered states had been and remained thugs and criminals. The Gestapo's secret police, answerable to no court or rule of law, were the worst.

Posters appeared with an endless list of regulations and restrictions, written in Norwegian and German. Hardly a lamppost or wall in Stavanger was spared. Of course, the inevitable graffiti followed: "Leve Kongen" ("Long live the King") and "Ned med Quisling" ("Down with Quisling, the traitor") were the most common. One night Ingolf and a friend rowed over to the island submarine base and stole a box of explosives. The next day Ingolf didn't pay any attention to a "verboten" sign when he went to check on the boat and a guard took him to the Gestapo headquarters. They telephoned the margarine plant and ordered them to send Ivar over immediately. If Ingolf had been much older than fourteen or it had been later in the war, he would have been in serious trouble. At this stage, the German attitude was still that they had come to the rescue of their Nordic cousins. Ivar, standing with hat in hand alongside Ingolf, listened to the officer's ranting and his demand at the end: "What are you going to do about it?" When Ivar shrugged his shoulders, the German shouted, "What do you think this is, a circus?" Ivar answered wistfully, "I wouldn't know. I have never been to a circus." In frustration at this simpleminded northerner, the German banged the desk with his fist. "Both of you. Get out of here and don't let me ever see you again." Ivar and Ingolf thanked their lucky stars as they hurried out of the dreaded building as fast as possible.

Ivar sent the unflappable Ingolf home and headed back to the plant. Greeted by his worried co-workers, he told them all about the meeting, amused that the Gestapo must be taking seriously the instructions given to every soldier on how to behave toward Norwegians. Everywhere, the contents were joked about. They stated that "certainly and regrettably, the Norwegians had no understanding of the aims of National Socialism, and therefore it was advisable to avoid discussing politics with them. But they might be won over by friendliness, by small attentions and by flattery. They were independent and undisciplined, and harsh orders would offend them; therefore it would be better to explain things to them in a simple matter-of-fact way or, still better, to adopt a playful tone. Their intelligence was a little slow, and they were suspicious of foreigners: therefore the benevolent German must not lose his temper, but take matters calmly" (Halvdan Koht, *Norway, Neutral and Invaded*). Ivar was deadly serious, however, when he called the boys together after supper and gave them a short lecture on staying out of trouble with the Germans. Ingolf was not paying much attention, Gunnar was wondering how to act if caught, and Jakob's mind was elsewhere, thinking about getting away with his friend, Peter. Ivar gave up and picked up the paper to read of new edicts.

Everyone aged fourteen to eighty was required to get identity cards with their photographs and the signatures of local officials. Rationing of bread, flour, butter, and fats had been introduced during the first month. Ivar's plant was forced to lay off some workers and cut back production of oleomargarine since fats were needed to make glycerin for explosives. Most of the margarine being made now went to the Germans. Ivar was concerned about the laid off workers, even though the Germans offered jobs to everyone at reasonable pay to build bunkers and fortifications. Once registered and in their clutches, he believed, the Germans would not let you leave. He had not counted on Ingolf, though. Ingolf was underage for heavy labor but got work as a "boy Friday" on island fortifications. After a few weeks, however, even the Germans had to concede defeat. He was too much of a goof-off and had other workers in stitches much of the time. Sent home, he arrived walking like Charlie Chaplin with two flapping left shoes. Gunnar asked "what happened?" Ingolf, puzzled, had no explanation. Ivar, with his inimitable sense of humor, told everyone to keep a sharp lookout for anyone else with brown and black shoes so they could swap.

Gunnar went out of his way to take on more chores for his mother, as she had to spend an increasing amount of time standing in shopping lines. He also spelled Marion in babysitting for Anna. That still left time to join a few friends to go into Stavanger, walk along the waterfront, and see what the Germans were doing. There were far fewer civilian cars on the road due to fuel restrictions but plenty of army vehicles, tanks, and horse–drawn wagons. By July, marching units incessantly sang "Wir Fahren Gegen Engelland" ("We're marching toward England"), and their invasion seemed to be a sure next step. The arrogance and confidence of the Germans was increasingly apparent, while Norwegian hopes were reaching their lowest point. The Germans could sing beautifully, however, and the boys enjoyed listening as they sat on the curb watching the soldiers march by.

Coincidentally, Norwegians began to take a great deal more interest in music after the German invasion, particularly their traditional folk songs. Mathilde and Ivar had a phonograph and purchased more Norwegian music for family gatherings and singing sessions. Ivar was reminded of Edvard Grieg saying, "I am sure my music has a taste of codfish in it." Bookstores and libraries experienced a surge of interest in cultural history and books in general. Norway had more bookstores per capita than any other nation. That and the fifty books per year lent on average to merchant seamen were proof of a more sophisticated people than Germany realized.

Reminders of the occupation increased daily. Alongside roads, utility poles and trees were painted with white bands so they could be seen during the blackouts. Street lamp globes were painted black except for narrow slits. Mathilde made sure every room had hooks over the windows for an extra cover in addition to the shades. In a neighboring village, a man sitting in his living room had been shot through the window by a German soldier who saw an edge of light at the side of his shade. Now every evening when Gunnar took Rex out for a walk, one of his chores was to circle the house and make sure no lights were showing. Fortunately sunset was not until almost ten o'clock, because electrical usage was cut back as well. This was quite a surprise to Ivar since Norway enjoyed a great amount of excess electricity before the war—in fact, 20 percent more per capita than any other European nation due to hydroelectricity from its many dams. Now monitors were being installed in homes. If your usage exceeded a set amount, 100 watts for example, lights would blink on and off until a bulb somewhere was unscrewed. The reason was war industry, particularly aluminum production. But a potential coal shortage was more of a concern for Ivar and Mathilde. The house was heated by small Franklin-like stoves in the corners of some first floor rooms that burned coke (coal with volatile gases baked out so it would burn hotter). By August conditions had not changed much, but after three months of occupation Mathilde was anxious to get away.

9

THE STEINSØY HARVEST

If you tickle the earth with a hoe she laughs

with a harvest.

—Douglas William Jerrold

T he last week in July the house was a beehive of activity as Mathilde made preparations to spend the whole month of August with her parents on Steinsøy. Only Ivar and Jakob would stay behind. Ivar would continue to work and take the ferry over on weekends. Jakob and his friend Peter were preparing to head into the mountains to escape the German labor conscription. Peter's family had relatives who owned a lumbering business deep in the rugged mountain region where the Germans would probably not be able to find them. They all left early Sunday morning. Mathilde took a taxi with Marion and Anna to the ferry terminal in Stavanger. Ivar, Gunnar, and Ingolf squeezed into the old Model T-powered skiff with Rex, the baggage, and a precious can of gasoline. Jakob helped them load and shook hands with everyone, then headed off with his backpack.

As usual, Mikal and Anna heard them coming and met them at the dock to help unload. An hour later Mathilde and Marion were whistling for someone to row over and pick them up from nearby Hundvag Island. Only the constant drone of airplanes in the distance reminded them of the German presence as they sat down for a Sunday dinner of sliced pork, homemade bread, creamed cabbage, and peas. Dessert was a choice of either freshly baked little cakes or berries picked that morning. Gunnar topped both with whipped cream. It was a wonderful change of scene. When it was time for Ivar to go, he decided it would be safer to leave the skiff at Steinsøy, and he put Gunnar in charge before being rowed over to Hundvag to catch the ferry. As Gunnar placed some extra fenders between the boat and dock and tied on fore and aft spring lines, he longingly eyed the engine. Someday.

A week later, the Roaldsøy family arrived for Sunday dinner from their island of the same name, a few miles north of Steinsøy. Five-year-old Nils, Mathilde's youngest sister's son, could hardly contain himself as he jumped out of their small sailboat to grab his cousin Gunnar around the legs. Gunnar was his favorite person in the entire world. Nils was the oldest of three children and although he had a few playmates on Roaldsøy, Gunnar was the one older boy who was willing to play with him and let him tag along. But first he had to tell Gunnar all about his exciting day when the Germans invaded, watching the Stuka dive bombers hurtling down with their distinctive ear-splitting howls. More than anything else in the world, he told Gunnar, he wanted to be a pilot when he grew up. Nils had been taken under the wing of the German officer commanding a fort being built on a nearby island, and he was also bursting to tell about his visits to the construction site.

Nils was still sticking to Gunnar later that afternoon when one of his uncles got everyone together for a family photograph. The uncle set up an old fashioned camera on the lawn, with tripod and black cloth to cover the head of the picture taker. In his navy blue Sunday suit, the portly uncle strode from side to side lining up the children in front and adults behind, all with great gusto and a steady supply of jokes. Several times he stepped back to review the setup and tug on the corners of his large walrus-like mustache. Finally he retreated twenty feet back and put the cloth hood over his head. "No!" he shouted. "Not quite right." Back he hustled to the group and moved two of the children a little closer. He repeated this a few more times, as the boys fidgeted and girls giggled. The adults stoically held their places. At last from under the hood he shouted, "Wonderful! Hold steady!" and pressed the button on the shutter cable. There was a brilliant flash and a loud explosion followed by smoke pouring out of the camera. It was all a hoax. It took a few seconds for it to sink in before everyone collapsed in laughter. At first, eighteen-month-old Anna started to cry but then joined in the merriment. It was a charming way to end an almost perfect day and to forget about the Germans.

Gunnar not only spent the summer helping with the normal farm chores but this year learned a whole range of building and maintenance skills from his grandfather. Strong from a lifetime of hard physical work, Mikal was always busy, and Gunnar had trouble keeping up with him. Ingolf was working in Stavenger most of the time, but Gunnar enjoyed being alone with his grandfather. Mikal was a master at woodworking and carpentry, which he had taught all the boys. Jakob turned out to be the best, but Gunnar took an acute interest in how to use tools and how things worked. The farm had electricity but no power tools. In his workshop, Mikal had an assortment of planes, chisels, saws, a bit and brace, several hammers, and screwdrivers. Gunnar's first lessons were on sharpening. He turned the crank on the large 1 1⁄2-inch thick stone grinding wheel and dripped water from a can in the other hand while his grandfather explained about correct angles and honing afterwards. One-third of a good woodworker's time is spent sharpening, he told Gunnar. But Gunnar had not stopped thinking about the boat engine, and of equal interest to him was metalworking with cold chisels, hacksaw, files, and drills. From working with his grandfather, he learned the lifelong lesson of patience and the reward of doing things right.

On the last weekend of harvesting, Nils returned to Steinsøy with his family and provided everyone with comic relief. Somehow he had got hold of an umbrella and, holding it open, jumped off the haystacks pretending to be a paratrooper. It was one of the few laughs that day as most of the afternoon was a scene of packing and tearful goodbyes. The future was not bright as the heavily loaded skiff left the dock for Hinna, with Rex again defiantly in the bow.

Gunnar started the fall school term in a converted private home, fifteen minutes away on a side street off the road to Stavanger. Desks, chalkboards, and supplies had been moved in during the summer. Ironically, his one new subject in the fifth grade was German, while English (soon to be banned) began in middle school. There were fewer students, as some families had left the region, but they were still packed cheek to jowl in the smaller rooms. This gave students more opportunity behind the teacher's back to poke each other or pull braids. Gunnar was one of the class favorites because he never teased. He would not back down from a bully and always came to the defense of the underdogs. This combination was not lost on his teachers who noted it in the gradebook he took home at the end of each term.

The food situation was getting worse. The farm on Steinsøy provided some help, but there were many mouths to feed in the Høynes family. Butter was no longer available except to those with cows. Chicory was introduced as a substitute for coffee. Sugar was very scarce, and the quality of bread and flour deteriorated substantially. The "New Bread," hard and flavorless, was made from "crisis" flour, undried wheat with sawdust. It caused flatulence and was jokingly referred to as *fisebrod* (fart bread). A Quisling party politician, in a speech praising Germany's National Socialism, unwittingly brought the house down with laughter when he spoke of a "new wind coming over Norway."

Then meat, eggs, and bacon just about disappeared and rutabagas became the meat substitute. Even fresh fish was difficult to get. The staples became dried stockfish, potatoes, and carrots along with rutabagas. Gunnar and other children in the neighborhood began to raise rabbits, but there were problems when their "pets" reached maturity. Swapping between families was one way to depersonalize the dish, but even that did not go over well in the Høines household so Mathilde had them give it up.

Thrifty Pea Soup: Put a pea into a large pot of
water. Bring to a boil. If the soup is too thick, throw
away the pea!
Norwegian recipe

In late September, the Germans dissolved the interim Norwegian Administrative Council they had set up to replace the king and parliament (Storting). With the revered Constitution abolished, Norway was now a vassal state and hope of semi-independence was gone. A perceptive friend of Ivar's, however, pointed out that German troops were no longer singing "Wir Fahren Gegen Engelland." A story soon went around about a boy asking a German soldier why they hadn't gone to England because his Viking ancestors used to go every summer.

A big boost for Ivar's morale, was the new 7:30 p.m. BBC Norwegian Service. Although listening to "enemy" broadcasts was prohibited and subject to fines and imprisonment, it was not strictly enforced at this stage of the war, and only Jews had been forced to turn in their radios. Gunnar joined his parents and Marion in the after-supper ritual of listening—but with one important difference from the old days. Tobacco rationing had begun. Ivar not only had to cut back his pipe smoking but the available Bulgarian brands were so awful and foul smelling that, in deference to Mathilde, he went outside for his few puffs after supper. No matter how bad, however, tobacco was soon worth its weight in gold and was used as the principal means of bartering for other goods. Personal columns in the newspaper were eagerly scanned for items to trade for tobacco. For most Norwegians this was the main reason to buy newspapers, which were highly censored and full of propaganda. The Lutheran Church had a long tradition of using chain letters, and a great deal of information about the war was now passed around this way, heavily laced with euphemisms—for example, news from England was referred to as "the West Wind."

The first Christmas under the occupation was a somber one. Not only was the weather the harshest in memory but most of the traditional dishes were no longer obtainable. Mathilde had been scrimping, saving, and bartering just to have the one meal with a little pork and lamb on Christmas Eve. At least the family was together again as Jakob had slipped home from logging in the mountains. Gunnar and Ingolf kept him up late into the night hours listening to his stories. Presents were not as plentiful as last year, but more thought and effort had been put into them. Gunnar was particularly touched that Jakob allowed him to use his ship model tools while he was away. They were kept in a small wooden replica of a sea chest where Jakob had never let anyone touch them. It was Jakob's principal hobby and he had become an expert. His latest work, an eighteen-inch model of a coastal steamer, was on display in the study and admired by every visitor. Several of his father's friends wanted to buy it. Gunnar made simple but solid wooden gifts in the basement at his father's workbench: a step stool for two-year-old Anna, a cookbook holder for his mother, and a pipe rack for Far. As the family gathered and held hands around the tree, Ivar reminded them how much they had to be thankful for considering the plight of the Poles and Jews and many other Norwegians. He had no inkling of the dramatic events in store for 1941, two turning points in the war: Hitler's decision to invade Russia and Japan's attack on Pearl Harbor.

THE LOW POINT

When it is dark enough, you can see the stars.

Charles A. Beard

The Germans continued to tighten their hold on Norway during the spring of 1941 by infiltrating and taking over the leadership of all important organizations, increasing rules, and brutally punishing even mild protests. Rationing was expanded and food supplies were further diminished. Mathilde was now spending up to four hours in shopping lines, and even dried fish and milk were getting scarce. To Gunnar, the most evident change was the almost universal conversion of vehicles from gasoline to carbon monoxide. It was generated by burning charcoal in external boiler-like tanks. Buses now had little pickup and could hardly climb the small hills around Stavanger. Often passengers had to be let off to lighten the load and help push. People learned to put a hand over the air intake at the bottom of the cylinder to hold the bus for latecomers. Only police, military, administrators, and doctors were permitted to use gasoline-powered vehicles. This included Dr. Høynes, who came by to check on the family but warned that food shortages were already causing malnutrition and lowering immunity to disease. Cases of tuberculosis and diphtheria were increasing dramatically.

Gunnar was interested and amused by the games that children invented. On a warm spring weekend, several neighborhood girls, about eight years old, set up a table outside arranged like a store counter. With make-believe ration books, they pretended to sell groceries. Gunnar approached them with his hand covering his mouth and whispered, "Do you have any coffee or butter?" The little shopkeeper glanced around furtively for signs of any *svina* (swine) before reaching under the table for a brown paper package. Gunnar laughed when he undid the wrapping only to find a fist-sized rock. They had acted out their various roles quite well. They even put on skits for him. One involved being caught and sent to prison and in another the children arranged escapes to Sweden. Gunnar was reminded of Nils jumping off the haystack with the umbrella, pretending it was a parachute. Children everywhere emulated what they saw and heard around adults. On his way home Gunnar began to think of other ways that disguises might be useful.

In June 1941 Ivar learned from listening to the BBC that Germany had invaded Russia. He could hardly believe it. Now, he felt, Hitler had finally bitten off more than he could chew and the Allies had a chance. His optimism did not last long, however, as the German panzer tanks raced deep into Russia, encircled whole armies, and took more than a million prisoners. Bad news soon followed on the home front. All radios except those belonging to the military, members of Quisling's NS party, and government officials had to be turned in over the next three months. Before the war, when radios were purchased they had to be registered with the state and an annual tax was paid to support Radio Norway. It was easy, therefore, for the Germans to find out who owned radios and track them down. But there was a loophole. Only one radio had to be listed on the tax rolls, so many stayed hidden in households with two or more sets. In any case, Germany was still winning almost everywhere and the authorities were not too concerned about illegal listening. It was more a ploy to increase membership in the NS party, though the result was quite disappointing for the Quislings.

The Høynes family had one radio set, and according to a posted schedule Ivar took it into Stavanger for a long wait in line. Gunnar's heart went out to his father. Two of the most enjoyable things in Far's life, a pipe in his favorite chair after supper and listening to the radio, were gone. They now took walks together with Rex after supper while Ivar had a few puffs on his pipe and talked about books. The family had a sizeable assortment in the living room. Mathilde liked the Will and Ariel Durant books the best while Ivar's taste was lighter. A current favorite was *How Green Was My Valley*, about a family of coal miners in Wales. He also like American Westerns he called "Bang Bangs."

Ingolf continued to court trouble. One evening after dark, he and a friend saw two soldiers sneaking a cigarette behind a fence. Walking past the other side, they spotted two submachine guns and backpacks lying on the ground. A nearby street lamp gave off just enough light to see the glistening barrels. Ingolf and his friend continued walking briskly for about a hundred feet and then doubled back, staying hidden by the fence. They picked up the two guns and tiptoed as fast as possible to a point where they could run without being heard. Minutes later and out of breath, they sat down behind a hedge to decide what to do with the guns. Faced with the reality of being shot if caught with them and unable to think of a good spot to hide them, they threw them under some nearby bushes and quickly headed for home. Ingolf told Gunnar about it when he got back and swore him to secrecy. His parents would have fits if they found out. All the next day at work, Ingolf could not stop thinking about the trouble the two soldiers would be in when they showed up without their weapons. He talked it over with Gunnar and they speculated about the possible results; German punishment would be brutal. It was a sobering thought and took a little away from their enjoyment of the prank.

Heroism consists in hanging on one minute longer.
Norwegian proverb

Gunnar woke up one night when he heard steps outside his door. Puzzled because Ingolf was spending the night away with a friend, Gunnar slipped out of bed and tiptoed to the door. When he heard Rex jumping around, he knew it was not a stranger. He opened the door and there was Jakob rummaging in the closet. Jakob put a finger to his lips and motioned for Gunnar to go back and sit on the bed with him. He had not shaved for days and his clothes were caked with dirt and mud. A German patrol had stopped him a few weeks back, and when his work papers turned out to be invalid for that district he was put in a labor battalion. He decided to escape when he heard his name and *borgevakt* duty mentioned at roll call. This meant he would have to guard a rail section, a bridge, or some other important post and if anything happened during his watch, he would be summarily executed. This system worked well for the Germans because Norwegians went overboard to avoid injuring their countrymen. Jakob told Gunnar that he just wanted to clean up, get some clothes, and head back to the mountains but needed to hurry and did not want to wake the family. He had a good reason for visiting surreptitiously. A brother would not notice but a mother would: Jakob's stomach was extended from malnutrition. After he shaved and put on clean clothes, Gunnar handed him a thick cheese sandwich as he headed out the back door. Gunnar tried to put the best face on things when he told his mother in the morning but she was clearly upset. She sensed something wasn't right.

Mathilde, Gunnar, Marion, and Anna spent almost two months that summer on Steinsøy helping farm, fish, and harvest. Ivar tended the garden at home after work and took the ferry over on weekends, while Ingolf picked up odd jobs around Stavanger. There were fewer visits from relatives to the island, but an increasing number of teenage boys came to court Marion, whose good looks and soft manner made her one of the more attractive girls around. Even the three German soldiers from the nearby island with the storage tanks tarried when they came over to buy eggs and milk, hoping to get a glimpse of her or even a word. Gunnar continued to improve his wood- and metalworking skills under his grandfather's guidance, but he did miss the company of other boys his age. One thing everyone missed was the sound of church bells. Bronze bells had been requisitioned for the war effort, and replacements made from other metals were slow in coming and did not have as pleasing a tone. When the family left the island after the August harvest, there was no improvement in the war news, just a steady stream of German advances on all fronts. Ivar was growing more and more despondent, but Mathilde, like most women, gritted her teeth, made do, and coped. No moping or self-pity for her.

In October 1941 came the first signs that the German war machine might be in for trouble. An edict was issued that each family must turn in one blanket for troops on the Russian front, where an early winter had set in. A payment by weight was established, but most families turned in their lightest and most threadbare possession and many refused on principle to accept the fairly nominal payment. (Though it was not made public until after the war, a special lightweight, windproof cloth the Germans had developed for the 1936 Winter Olympic Games and supplied to many of the troops turned out to have hardly any insulating properties when wet.) Two months later, each family was ordered to turn in a rucksack. These were small nuisances compared to the increasingly aggressive attempts by the new Minister of Churches and Education to promote the Nazi's "New Order" philosophy. One of his first acts had been to eliminate English in schools. When the churches were forced to promote National Socialism, the Lutheran leadership resigned, resulting in a mass boycott of services.

Equally disturbing were the storm trooper-like members of the Hird who put down student dissent in Oslo by invading the university with clubs. The color red was now considered a show of support for Communism, and Hird members roamed the streets snatching off and confiscating *nisselue,* the pointed elf-like caps with tassels, and other articles of red clothing. One student was stripped and whipped for wearing a paperclip in his lapel, a symbol that stood for "We are holding together." Other resistance symbols were a matchstick in the hat band for "We are enlightened," and a capital "H" with a "7" inserted for King Haakon VII painted on walls and over posters.

Gunnar and the Høines family saw little evidence of the Quislings or Hird members in Stavanger, compared to what they heard was going on in Oslo. Without a university student population there were far fewer incidents to incite retaliation. Ivar and thousands of others, however, had participated in one of Norway's most moving and effective protests the previous December. Slowly and silently, they walked three or four abreast in two columns on either side of the road from the Eiganes area to downtown Stavanger. The watching Germans knew they were dealing with a very resolute and unusual people.

Earlier that fall, Ivar got hold of a duckling to fatten for Christmas and Gunnar helped build a pen in the back yard. The duckling kept escaping, and after innumerable chases around the neighborhood Mathilde got fed up and insisted it be taken to Steinsøy to stay with the small flock of chickens there. The duck was there but a few weeks when it escaped again and was shot while swimming across to the adjacent island. Mikal had heard one of the soldiers there shooting at it and told Ivar and the family the story at Sunday dinner. Gunnar said nothing, but when he got up from the table he went straight down to the dock and rowed across to confront the Germans. He marched right up to the farmhouse, knocked at the door, and went in. Three surprised Germans in their suspenders were sitting around the kitchen table playing cards. Gunnar right away let them have a piece of his mind. "You shot a duck you knew belonged to my grandparents and it was going to be their Christmas dinner," he said. "What kind of soldiers would steal from old people who have treated you so well? You ought to be ashamed of yourselves." The Germans were too taken aback to say a word and stared in amazement at this eleven-year-old speaking so forcefully. These were "fortress battalion" soldiers, older men in defensive units, not fanatic members of the brutal Waffen SS. They sheepishly shrugged their shoulders. Gunnar turned and headed back to his boat as fast as he dared. Arriving at the family dock, he told his worried grandfather and parents what he had done. Mikal's eyes shone with pride, but Ivar and Mathilde could only shake their heads. A few days later, one of the soldiers rowed over with a bar of chocolate and apologized to Mikal and Anna. He rolled his eyes when he asked about "that boy."

11

NORWAY, HITLER'S "ZONE OF DESTINY"

Unqualified security in the Northern area

is more important than a new spring offensive

against the Soviet Union.

Hitler, November 1942, speaking about Norway

On Monday morning December 8, 1941, Mathilde was setting out breakfast and planning her day for the never-ending holiday cleaning ritual when the phone rang. A neighbor excitedly blurted out news of a Japanese attack on the United States the evening before. People were speculating about what effect this would have on the European war, she said. Three days later, to the surprise of many, Germany declared war on the United States, and most Norwegians were sure from then on that the Allies would win. So many Norwegians had relatives or friends in the United States that America's strength and capabilities were well known. There was even talk of the war ending in a matter of months; hardly anyone thought it would last three and a half more years. There was a new spirit that Christmas, even though the only foods not rationed were dried fish, vegetables, and fruit. Ivar, hoping to make up for the lost duck, got hold of a sheep's head which Mathilde furtively spent hours preparing. When carried in to the dining room on a platter, though, the children exchanged horrified glances. Even Rex growled when he saw it. The two eyes seemed to stare reproachfully at each diner in turn, and except for Mathilde and Ivar, the children just silently poked at the slices before them. Halfway through the meal, Mathilde took the sheep's head back to the kitchen. She was already thinking about salvaging it for soups and stews.

Two days after Christmas, while the Høynes family made the traditional round of holiday visits, British Commando raids were taking place farther north that would have a profound influence on Norway and the course of the war. On Christmas day, German intelligence had told Hitler that the United States and Britain were planning a much larger operation in Norway the following spring. Hitler called an emergency staff meeting on December 29. His staff's best guess was that the British raid was a probing action to prepare for the spring invasion. Designating Norway the "Zone of Destiny," Hitler immediately ordered substantial troop reinforcements and upgraded the coast artillery. He not only made this a higher priority than the planned spring Russian offensive but ordered all capital ships (battleships and cruisers) concentrated in Norway as well.

Partly out of fear of the Allies' return and paranoia about an internal uprising, in January 1942 the Germans interned twenty-four of the most prominent Norwegians considered still loyal to the king and government in exile. One of these "court hostages" was Odd Nansen, the architect son of the late Fridtjof Nansen, famed arctic explorer, diplomat, and humanitarian. The senior Nansen had without doubt been Norway's most revered citizen. He helped further the country's independence from Sweden in 1905 and won the Nobel Peace Prize in 1922 for his relief work saving children in Russia and Germany after World War I. Odd Nansen continued his father's work as head of the children's relief agency. Ivar, like most Norwegians, was appalled at his imprisonment since many German children had been rescued by that agency and taken into Norwegian homes. An older couple in the neighborhood had stayed in contact with one of them, now a German soldier, who had come to Norway as a five-year-old in 1920. They had brought up the German boy alongside their own son. His 1939 Christmas postcard said he had been promoted to corporal and wished them good health and peace. Gunnar listened to his father tell the story and wondered how he would react if he were in his neighbor's place and his former guest showed up at the door in uniform. Many stories circulated about German children, sheltered years ago, coming back as tourists to spy on Norway's defenses.

> *But good God, people don't do such things!*
> Henrik Ibsen, *Hedda Gabler*

In 1942, several of the war's most brutal reprisals occurred. In February, an informer tipped off the Germans that a boat holding twenty-three refugees headed for England was about to leave Alesund, a coastal town halfway between Bergen and Trondheim. All were captured and their leader executed. Under torture, twenty more people were implicated, arrested, and sent to Stavanger for trial. A little more than a month later, two British agents put ashore on the island of Televaag near Bergen were betrayed and discovered hiding in a farmhouse. In the ensuing shootout, two German officers were killed before the wounded British were captured. In retaliation, all three hundred houses on the island were burned to the ground, cattle and livestock killed or confiscated, and all the fishing boats sunk. Seventy-six men aged sixteen to sixty-five were sent to German concentration camps, many never to survive, and the remaining 260 women, children, and old men were interned in Norwegian prisons. One British agent died of wounds and the other was tortured and executed, along with a local resistance leader. Not content with these punishments, Joseph Terboven, the German Reichskommissar, ordered eighteen prisoners from the Alesund affair executed as examples even though they had no involvement with the Televaag shooting. An entire nation was horrified.

Ivar and most Norwegians could not believe that Germany, a "civilized" nation, could do such things. But the last straw, which ended any chance to win over the Norwegian people, was an order that all teachers join a new "Teacher's Front" union created by the NS party. Out of 14,000 teachers, 12,000 sent identical letters rejecting the order. Furious, the government arrested 290 in Oslo, 200 in Bergen, and another 900 from the rest of Norway so every district would be taught a lesson. Of these, 700 were immediately sent to a special punishment camp. They spent twenty-seven hours jammed into cattle trucks without food or water and then lived in virtual hell for three weeks. Only 50 of the teachers recanted. After weeding out the sick and the elderly, the remaining 500 were literally packed like sardines in the bottom holds of a coastal steamer for the long journey around the North Cape to arctic prison conditions at Kirkenes. They spent five months there.

Norwegians were infuriated to see civic leaders and respected citizens treated like common criminals. This was particularly true in small towns and settlements that until then had been relatively untouched by the occupation. Schools were closed for a month before the government backed down in a humiliating defeat, but the damage was irreparable. The entire nation was unified. Gunnar used the break from school to watch Hitler's overreaction to the Commando raids: many more soldiers and vehicles, but of greater interest to Gunnar were the construction sites with their steam shovels, cranes, and bulldozers.

12

THE RESOURCEFUL BOYS

There is always one moment in childhood when the

door opens and lets the future in.

Graham Greene, *The Power And The Glory*

ne morning after chores, Gunnar took his bicycle to see what was happening at an anti-aircraft flak tower being built on a hill west of Hinna. He walked half the way to conserve his much patched and very thin tires, which were impossible to replace. He had tightly wound a layer of twine around a particularly worn section but had not reached the point of using a thick rope for a tire like Jakob or threading a string through corks as some friends did. Gunnar got within a hundred feet of the tower site and propped the bike against a tree. He walked partly around the perimeter marked by a makeshift fence with "Verboten" signs every thirty or so feet warning civilians to stay away.

One of the main reasons Gunnar had come, and other onlookers too, was to see the newly arrived prisoners they had heard about. All the prisoners, in shabby vertical-striped uniforms, had shaved heads and were emaciated. They worked slowly and methodically, but occasionally Gunnar would see a guard shouting at prisoners who were forced to run "at the double" as punishment. Gunnar could not stand to watch for more than a few minutes, and he was heading home when he noticed a small metal canister on a tarp next to an unguarded truck, along with some rolls of wire and stakes. He glanced around, and seeing no guard looking his way, reached down and picked it up. Shielding it with his body, he examined it. He could not tell what it was used for, but it had an outlet for an electrical plug and his curiosity about mechanical things surfaced. When he got home he showed it to Jakob, who was back for a few days from his mountain retreat. Jakob had never seen anything like it either, so they got an extension cord to test it. When they connected the cord to a wall outlet, the canister emitted an ear-splitting siren-like alarm. It did not stop when they pulled the plug. The last thing Jakob wanted was for the police or military show up and ask the dreaded "Ausweiss, bitte" ("Your papers, please."). In a panic, he and Gunnar raced into the kitchen and plunged the canister into a pail full of water. It worked! The screeching alarm stopped. That night, Gunnar hid the canister under his jacket, and down at the communal dock he threw it off the end. Later, he and Jakob laughed about it. For the life of them, they could not figure out why it wouldn't stop.

They had a much better laugh when Ingolf got home from work. Through one of his great uncle's connections, Ingolf had been working at a sardine factory in Stavanger the last few months, and both Ivar and Mathilde crossed their fingers hoping he would stay out of trouble there. During supper, Mathilde could tell Ingolf was up to something. He was just bursting to get away from the table and tell Jakob about an escapade he and a friend had pulled off earlier in the day. Mathilde knew she would find out sooner or later from Marion and figured it couldn't be too bad if Ingolf was holding in laughter. Gunnar was also anxious to hear what was going on and followed Jakob and Ingolf up to the attic. There, Ingolf collapsed on the bed holding his sides. Finally, Jakob threatened to leave if he did not calm down and tell them what happened.

For the last few days, Ingolf and a friend at work had been discussing a prank they wanted to pull, and they decided to go ahead during the lunch period when the other workers left the building to eat and talk. Ingolf and his buddy scooped up buckets of decaying fish heads at the receiving and processing section and carried them over to the canning line where they sealed the heads in large tins for shipment to Germany. Their factory's name was not on the labels, so they felt reasonably safe. On the way home, the boys nearly collapsed in hysterics as they imagined the scene in German households when people opened their "Product of Norway" sardines to see dozens of decaying fish eyes looking up at them from the stinking mess. Jakob and Gunnar conjured up other hilarious scenarios until Marion came up and had to be let in on the secret. The boys were still chuckling when the lights were turned out.

> *Light thickens, and the crow makes wing to the*
> *rooky wood.*
> Shakespeare, *Macbeth*

Ivar had not been idle in looking for food. Through a "friend of a friend" he was able to buy an aged Norwegian Fjord Horse, quite a bit smaller but far more agile in mountainous Norway than the German plow variety. Ivar asked a local butcher, who took part of it in payment, to cut it into manageable pieces for canning and salting. Mathilde did not tell the children, storing it discretely in the basement in a wooden keg and jars. It was stringy and tough, but Mathilde was by necessity becoming more and more creative in making almost any bit of protein palatable, even crows.

In front of the house grew two tall fir trees where hundreds of large crows roosted. One day Mathilde asked Gunnar if they could catch or trap them somehow. Gunnar thought about it for awhile. He could never sneak up on them, but he told Mor that if he got in the tree while the crows were out scavenging and waited for them to come back to roost in the early evening, he might be able to grab one. The next day just before dusk, Gunnar scrambled up a tall ladder that he and Mor set against the tree trunk. He crawled out on a large branch and, stretched out in a prone position, waited motionless for what seemed hours. Finally, a large crow landed close enough for Gunnar to grab one of its legs and pull it flapping to his chest. He wrung its neck before dropping it down to his mother. The commotion caused other birds to take off, but Gunnar waited patiently for ten more minutes and was able to grab another and toss it down to Mor. It was getting dark so he climbed down and put away the ladder, feeling quite a sense of accomplishment. Mathilde had to do some sustained pounding with a mallet to tenderize the tough breasts, but thinly sliced, pan-fried, and mixed with chopped cabbage, they were a welcome change in the family's very limited diet.

Gunnar periodically got out the ladder to grab another crow or two when his mother was running low on other protein.

> *You should never have your best trousers on when*
> *you go out to fight for freedom and truth.*
> Henrik Ibsen, *An Enemy of the People*

Creativity was necessary not just in the kitchen, but in all aspects of life. Gunnar's mother made soap out of tallow, cod liver oil, potash from ashes, and caustic soda. This was cooked over the stove and Gunnar helped by slowly stirring the mixture. Every bit of clothing was patched and re-patched. There was no leather to resole worn out shoes. One solution was to tan the tough part of a cod's skin for the uppers, which was then nailed to wooden soles with slots sawed across them to give some flexibility. These shoes were not long lasting nor were clothes made with the new synthetic cloth derived from cellulose in wood products, as Ingolf soon discovered. One hot and humid day Ingolf arrived home from work in a newly purchased blue suit and white shirt with tie. When he took off his jacket, Marion and Gunnar burst out laughing. His white shirt had a dark blue "V" line where the lapels had been. Below, there was a bluish tint down to the belt line. Moisture in the cellulose-based threads had caused the dye to ooze out.

Ingolf gave up on the blue suit with the leaking dye and decided instead to do some fix-up tailoring of his own. One Saturday afternoon he borrowed scissors, needle, and thread from his mother and disappeared upstairs to his room. About an hour later, the family was gathered around talking when Ingolf appeared on the stair landing with a big grin and announced, "What do you think?" He was a most unusual sight, and it took the family a minute to realize what he had done before the laughter started. His pants were inside out, white muslin pockets hanging in full view. Ingolf continued his fashion show at the bottom of the stairs, demonstrating how he had to reach down inside the front of his trousers to pull up the zipper. Two year old Anna laughest the hardest. It was quite comical, and Ivar suggested that Ingolf coordinate the pants with the one brown and one black shoe and the white shirt with the blue "V."

13

ENCOUNTERS WITH
THE GERMANS

If only one had the Viking spirit in life.

Ibsen, *The Master Builder*

ince Ivar was one of the few workers at the margarine plant with a
driver's license, he was often called upon to drive the company truck
for deliveries to German installations. The truck had been converted
to using carbon monoxide gas generated by burning blocks of wood,
and it had the usual problems making it up hills. This was an ideal
setup for Ivar. He would let some friends know his route in advance
so they could pick a hill and stand by waiting for the truck to pass.
A German guard always rode in the passenger seat, but the natural
slowing on the hill was not suspicious. Ivar, looking out the rear view
mirror, would slow down just a bit more for his friends to run up behind and grab a few tubs of margarine. Since they had not stopped,

the puzzled guard could not account for the missing tubs when the truck arrived at its destination. Ivar did not dare do this too often.

On the other hand, Ingolf and his friend were caught by the foreman canning more decayed fish heads. Deathly afraid of the German reaction if discovered and dubious about Ingolf's ability to stay out of further trouble, the manager sacked them both. This time Ivar went to his friend at the Victoria Hotel and asked him as a special favor to take on Ingolf as a *pikkolo,* a combination servant and errand boy. The job had a very low salary but it came with a uniform and meals. Ingolf was hired.

Though the summer of 1942 was relatively uneventful for the family, food and other items became more scarce. Gunnar spent most of his time on Steinsøy with his mother, Anna, and Marion. Again he learned a lot from his grandfather while working on the farm. Ivar made one trip across to Skudenes to check on his parents and came back with some sad news. He had made a side visit to the Isaksens and found little three-year-old John without his mother. She had been interned in Grini concentration camp near Oslo along with other so-called "enemy aliens." There was good news from Jakob, however. He was still safe and cutting wood in the mountains although anxious to join the resistance when old enough. Marion was blossoming, and Gunnar, playing the role of escort, would row over to the big island and walk with her to the local soccer club for the Saturday evening dances. A pianist played foxtrots and waltzes, usually accompanied by a fiddle and an accordion. Gunnar was not particularly interested in girls yet, but for the occasional folk dances he would politely go down the line asking wallflowers to be his partner. Gunnar was saddened to see the quite prominent use of homemade alcohol by some of the older boys and young men; it often resulted in fistfights. He and Marion usually missed this. They left early because Mikal and Rex were always at the dock waiting for them. Some miles away on the outskirts of Stavanger there was a small hall called the Match Box where patrons jammed in like sardines could dance the whole evening for the equivalent of twenty–five cents. Jakob often kicked up his heels there but not with wallflowers. The more attractive girls would not let go of him.

Ingolf could not avoid trouble or pass an opportunity to get even with the Germans but he led a charmed life. One very hot summer day after work, he was taking a walk along the fjord shoreline in the neighboring village of Vaulen when he saw a group of five or six German soldiers taking a swim in a cove with a small sandy beach. Their neatly piled uniforms were about fifteen feet in from the water and Ingolf could see the edges of some pistol belts under the top layers. The soldiers were splashing water at each other, laughing, and having fun. Ingolf moved closer to the uniforms and when the soldiers were looking the other way he snatched two pistols from their holsters. Just as he was putting them inside his shirt and turning to walk away there was a shout, :"halt", followed by a stream of swear words in German.

Ingolf had a good start toward a nearby grove of woods when three of the soldiers in their wet underpants raced out of the water after him. Running as fast as he ever had in his life, Ingolf, without turning, threw one of the pistols back over his shoulder. This instinctive move probably saved him. The soldiers thinking he had taken just one pistol stopped to retrieve it while Ingolf disappeared deep in the woods. With his heart pounding, he hid for some time to make sure they didn't follow or spot him. He very cautiously took a roundabout way back home and went in the back cellar entrance after making sure no one saw him. After going up to his room and putting the pistol under his pillow, Ingolf relaxed and laughed while thinking of HItler's "master race" cursing and running barefooted after him in their "undies."

That night he showed the pistol to Jakob. It was a long-barreled automatic fire machine model, which they proceeded to take apart. For the life of them, they could not get it back together and it was thrown off the dock the next evening.

Gunnar was all ears when Ingolf arrived at Steinsøy with his father and told him the story. Gunnar knew he was a big help on the island, but talking with Ingolf made him anxious to get home where all the "action" was. After he returned to Hinna and started a new school term, he looked forward to suppers when Ingolf told of events at the hotel and passed on gossip. Gunnar's after-supper walks with his father and Rex, however, were marred by the reduced tobacco supply. When Far was completely out and fidgeting with an empty pipe, Gunnar wracked his brain wondering how he could possibly get hold of some more. A neighbor friend said they should have grown some like his uncle on a mountain farm up near Trondheim. Ivar's friend laughed, though, when he received a letter from his aunt reporting that goats had broken through a protective fence and eaten all the tobacco. For three straight days, the uncle sat staring morosely at the empty patch in a state of withdrawal. Every so often, he got up and threw rocks at the goats.

> *Bait the hook well! This fish will bite.*
> Shakespeare, *Much Ado About Nothing*

Lying in bed one night, Gunnar was remembering the game of grocery store played by the neighborhood girls when he had an idea. Sunday, when most of the Germans had the day off (a practice peculiar to Norway and stopped by an irate general in 1945), Gunnar took a large round turnip and coated it with a thin layer of margarine. He wrapped it tightly in cellophane, exactly like a ball of butter. The large ship basin in front of the Victoria Hotel was a favorite place for German soldiers to promenade with their girlfriends during holidays. It was sunny autumn weather, so Gunnar headed there to try his luck. He was hardly off the bus when he spotted a German officer with a girl on his arm and a cigarette in his free hand. The officer seemed friendly, smiling and talking as he strolled along. Gunnar hurried over to show him the "butter" ball and asked, "Tobacco?" The soldier nodded and took a pack of cigarettes from his pocket. He shook out a few to keep and handed the pack to Gunnar. Gunnar gave him the "butter" ball and started to hurry away, but the girlfriend stepped forward with a small bar of chocolate in her hand for the "cute looking boy," she said. Flustered, Gunnar shook his head and ran. Later he thought they both probably had a good laugh at being taken in by the young Norwegian. At home, he gave the cigarettes to Far, who asked no questions. Far stripped off the paper and mixed the real tobacco with chopped, dried berry leaves to stretch the hoard. His spirits picked up noticeably.

Mathilde, in the meantime, had come up with a new dish. She very thinly sliced some kalrabi, a variety of turnip, and pan-fried it until it was golden brown. The first night she tried it on the family, Ivar said, "Tilda, my princess. This is quite nice." The second night, it was, "Tilda, my princess. This is not so bad." The third night, with a quizzical look Ivar asked, "Tilda, my dove. Doesn't it taste a little

Marion and Anna, circa 1943

funny?" The fourth night, after one bite, Ivar, forgetting to add an in-dearment said plaintively, "Tilda! I hate it!" Pretending to be peeved, Mathilde responded, "Far! Since you have never been in the kitchen, make an appointment and I will show you where it is and give you a tour. Then you can pick out things you like." Ivar meekly finished his plate. Gunnar and the other children hid their smiles. They could not recall ever seeing their father in the kitchen—not that Mathilde would want him underfoot.

14

DECEMBER 1942:
THE TURNING POINT

The loser of this war will be the side that

makes the greatest blunders.

Hitler

uring October and November 1942, more dire punishments were posted for infractions, including the death penalty for listening to foreign broadcasts. The Gestapo and police began rounding up the Norwegian Jewish population in October. First men were arrested, and then a month later women and children. Quick action by the resistance, humanitarian groups, and individual Norwegians helped half of the Jews escape to Sweden over the next several months. They took a great many risks hiding the Jews and arranging transportation to staging posts near the border. From there Jews made dramatic dashes the last mile or so to escape German patrols. Those interned were sent in groups, as shipping became available, to the Auschwitz death camp in Germany. By the end of February 1943, the last shipment was made. Only about 24 survived out of the 760 sent.

The vast majority of Jews lived in Oslo and Trondheim, so Stavanger was hardly affected. Still, Ivar knew of three Jewish families, all owners of small downtown shops. One of them was telephoned and warned by a neighboring merchant that the Gestapo were hanging around outside his shop and he had better stay away. He took a chance and was last seen being beaten and dragged into a police car. Within minutes, the Gestapo looted his shop and sealed it off. Like most Norwegians, Ivar had virtually no prejudice, and he abhorred violence. This injustice against a man that he knew had a deep impact on Ivar, with his strong sense of decency and fairness. He was not one to express outrage visibly, and he told his family about the incident quietly, but with obvious distress. Mathilde was concerned about the occasional look of hopelessness she saw in her husband's eyes despite word of German setbacks that were filtering in from different fronts. By mid-December, Ingolf was hearing more gossip at the hotel about a potential disaster in Russia. An entire German army was surrounded at a place called Stalingrad, and people were talking about an unusually harsh Russian winter. There were also rumors of a major German retreat in Africa, but perhaps the biggest news was an American landing in Morocco. Norwegians would never have guessed, based on German-controlled radio and censored newspapers, that the fortunes of war had turned. In movie theaters, the mass of propaganda in the documentaries and shorts kept most Norwegians away. But this gave Gunnar the opportunity to start his arsenal.

Gunnar, now twelve years old, often went to one of Stavanger's three theaters on Sunday to see the three o'clock movie. The audiences were small, except when a Swedish or an occasional American film was shown. There were always a number of German officers in attendance with their side arms and female companions. Since there was plenty of room, they usually placed their pistol belts and holsters on an empty seat next to them. Gunnar observed this, and for several weeks he had been considering the risks of stealing a pistol. One Sunday morning he recalled the neighborhood game the little girls played with the rock wrapped in paper and decided to take a chance. He found a rock that would fit a holster and put it in a brown paper lunch bag. Standing alone in the back of the theater, he looked over the audience for an empty seat behind a German officer with a gun belt visible on the seat next to him and his date on the other side. Several seats met the criteria, and Gunnar picked the one closest to the back that offered a quick getaway and had less light from the screen. In the seat behind the holster, he waited.

The movie came to a particularly romantic scene with a long drawn-out kiss and swelling music. The German soldier turned and nuzzled his girl. Gunnar reached over, slipped the pistol gently from its holster, and substituted the rock, all in the space of a few seconds. He placed the pistol inside the bag and carefully tiptoed out of the row. Once in the aisle, he hurried out of the theater, hoping no one would pay attention to a twelve-year-old boy riding home on the bus with a small package. Arriving home, he went straight to the basement with the pistol. It was a P-38 with a clip full of bullets. He hid the pistol in an old wooden box in the basement and placed some garden supplies on top. Gunnar's stomach churned when he thought of the danger involved in stealing it but he felt better thinking of the German opening his holster and finding a rock.

I am very fond of pigs; but I don't find it
difficult to eat them.
Robert Runcie, Archbishop of Canterbury

After last year's disaster with the sheep's head for Christmas,
Ivar went in with a neighbor on a fifty-fifty deal to buy a piglet on
the black market. They hid it in the neighbor's basement for several
months to fatten it up. A week before Christmas, Ivar went over on a
Saturday with Gunnar to help slaughter it. Neither would ever forget.
The neighbor had a large mallet to knock the pig unconscious, but
once out of its straw-floored pen the pig raced around the square
brick column in the center of the basement. It was impossible to
corner, and it let out ear-piercing screams and baby-like howls after each glancing blow. The neighbor was cross-eyed and Ivar could
hardly contain himself watching the wayward whacks at the pig.
Hurrying so as to avoid alerting the whole neighborhood, they were
finally able to catch the pig, truss it up by the hind legs, and slit its
throat. Perspiring profusely and covered with blood, they sat down
exhausted and decided they would never do that again. Ivar withheld
the gory details from the family, but a few weeks later he told them
about the chase. He got everyone laughing by imitating the cross-
eyed neighbor's missed swipes with the mallet.

The Christmas Eve dinner was a wonderful reminder of better
times. More relatives than usual came when word got around about
the traditional "villa pig" raised for this occasion. While Ivar led a
prayer of thanks for the bounty of the delicious sliced pork, it did
cross his mind that another neighbor's German Shepherd had not
been seen for over a week. He could not be critical, though; after all,
Roald Amundsen, the nation's explorer hero, reached the South Pole
in 1911 ahead of Britain's Scott because of his calculated consump-

tion of sled dogs along the way. Gunnar once again built presents in the basement using his father's carpentry tools and was responsible for the *nisse* platter and bundle of wheat for the birds. This year, he did not try to keep the *nisse's* plate from Rex. "The heck with folktales and scary stories of what an unhappy *nisse* might do," he thought. Rex had been suffering just like everyone else. Didn't those little elves know there was a war on?

15

THE VICTORIA HOTEL

Grab a chance and you won't be sorry for a

might-have-been.

Arthur Ransome

The most important event at the beginning of 1943 was the fate of the German 6th Army at Stalingrad. Of the original 285,000 men, 90,000 had surrendered by February 2 and only about 5,000 ever reached their homeland years later. Rumors about the impending disaster had circulated for weeks, and Hitler tried to put the best face on it by claiming the soldiers had fought to the last man in the glorious tradition of the German Army. Russian newsreels, however, showed long columns of unshaven, emaciated prisoners trudging off to Siberia holding pieces of blood stained blankets against the 30-degrees-below-zero blizzard conditions. These pictures shattered the myth of

The Victoria Hotel

German invincibility throughout much of the world. Norwegians saw none of them, but the three days of official mourning and the radio's repeated playing of the last movement of Beethoven's Fifth Sympathy let them know something monumental had occurred.

Each evening the family could hardly wait for Ingolf to get home and tell them what news he picked up at the hotel. Like many Norwegians, Ingolf had had a few years of German in school and after two years hearing the language spoken during the occupation, he could understand most of what he overheard at work. He noticed the officers were now talking more quietly in small groups and stopped or changed the subject when a hotel worker came near. They glanced around frequently during conversations. Ingolf also heard remarks about punishment for "defeatist" remarks or attitude. The Gestapo and their brothers in the Waffen SS military units were becoming even more fanatical in reporting on their fellow Germans. Gunnar did not dare pass on to his friends anything he heard at home. He had heard what happened in Alesund and Televaag because of an informer, and the subsequent tortures and executions in Stavanger had an indelible impact. A recent outrage involved a woman Ivar knew slightly. Ivar, in a tearful voice, could barely tell the family that Solveig Bergslien, the office manager of the municipal jail, committed suicide during Gestapo interrogation. She had an important role in the resistance and had been informed on but she died without revealing names. This had a tremendous effect on Gunnar. He wanted to do something more important than attend school and run errands at home.

Gunnar, now thirteen, pleaded with his parents to let him take a job like Ingolf when the term was over. He wanted to earn money for the family and, with luck, bring home some fringe benefits like Ingolf's—a little leftover food or some chocolate as a tip for running a special errand. Little did he know that he would take Ingolf's place at the hotel for the next two years. Ingolf's outgoing and upbeat personality brought him to the attention of Axel Lund's wife, Ellen, who increasingly called on him to run personal errands and even acompany her on short social and business trips. More bothersome for Ingolf was her unpredictable schedule which caused him to miss soccer practice and games. He decided to change jobs and talked it over with his father. Ivar then asked Gunnar if he might be interested in taking Ingolf's place. It was exactly the chance Gunnar had been waiting for and after many months of stories from Ingolf at dinner, he was familiar with the duties at the hotel and anxious to give it a try. Ivar called his friend at the hotel about Ingolf's decisions and asked if he might bring Gunnar in for an interview.

The following day, Ivar took Gunnar in for an interview during the lunch hour. Gunnar made an especially good impression and was hired after fifteen minutes of questions and an introduction to Mr. Lund. Axel Lund took an instant liking to this clean cut, exceptionally polite boy who looked him straight in the eye and did not hesitate to speak up. Ingolf was quite pleased to gracefully leave the hotel on good terms and on his last day went out of his way to break in Gunnar, giving him a tour of the hotel, introducing him to all the staff, and explaining his basic duties. Gunnar was fitted out for the dark blue uniform, a high-necked brass buttoned jacket with pants to match and a military-style cap with a narrow bill. The hotel seamstress had the alterations finished the next day when he reported for work.

Much of Gunnar's time was spent on errands for the manager and Mr. Lund, but he also helped carry bags and did odd jobs. He was kept busy and got to know just about everyone on the staff within a few weeks. The food was decent, mostly what was left over from the officers' meals, and occasionally Gunnar was able to take a bit home. The hotel had one elevator, wide front stairs that wound up and around the elevator shaft, and back stairs on either side of the hotel. The fifth floor with its low ceilings was primarily used for storage, with some dormer rooms for staff. One large reception room on the second floor had been converted into a buffet breakfast room, while the original main restaurant to the left of the entrance lobby served as the officer's mess for dinner. There was a great scarcity of hotel accommodations for commercial visitors to Stavanger, and the Victoria became the main information center for available rooms in private homes. Giving visitors directions and sometimes helping carry their luggage for short distances was a good source of tips, usually money but often chocolate or a cigarette or two. What Gunnar really wanted, though, was the radio he had spotted in one of the rooms.

One day during the first month of work, Gunnar was walking along the third floor corridor after bringing a bag up to an officer's room when he happened to glance in the open doorway of a room being cleaned by a chamber maid. On the bedside table was a radio just about the same size as the one his parents had turned in a year ago. Gunnar paused for a moment before continuing down to the lobby, but the thought of getting a radio for his father would not go away. He had committed the room number to memory, and for the rest of the day and on the way home he considered all the ways he could get in the room, take the radio out, and get it home. A week passed. Then one morning while taking trash out back, he saw the solution. He had hardly a moment to think about his discovery when to his horror and disgust a large rat ran up his side to his neck and down his sleeve. He lashed out his arm to throw it off. The rat hit against the brick wall and scurried under the trash pile while Gunnar bolted toward the back door.

16

THE RADIO

Audacity augments courage; hesitation, fear.

Publilius Syrus, *Moral Sayings*

What Gunnar saw on the pile of trash in the backyard was an empty corrugated liquor carton designed to hold four bottles for mailing. It was the perfect size for the radio, and when he returned to the lobby he began thinking about how and when to go for the prize. Around noon, when almost all of the Germans were gone, he waited until the clerk at the reception desk stepped away for a trip to the men's room and went behind the desk. He took the master key off its hook and quickly headed out back to the trash area. He had no problem taking the box up the back stairs and getting into the room. But once inside, having closed the door behind him, Gunnar had a strange, eerie feeling. Like most of the rooms, this one had a large photograph of the occupant in full military regalia proudly displaying his medals and decorations. Undoubtedly a duplicate was displayed in a prominent place at home in Germany. The particularly stern eyes of the officer in the frame on the dresser seemed to follow Gunnar as he crossed the room. It bothered him so much that he had to stop and turn the picture face down before he could go on. He knelt to unplug the radio and was just about to put it in the box when he heard the sound of boot steps outside in the hall. Even on the soft carpeting, he could tell it was a German by the distinctive military stride.

Gunnar froze. His mind raced thinking about what to do if the German was heading for the same room. Only two ideas came to him. Hiding under the bed was one, which he quickly rejected. It would take time to reconnect the radio and he might have to stay hidden for hours. In a flash he decided to stand close to the door and throw the radio in the face of whoever opened it. That might give him a chance to duck past and escape down the back stairs. Leaning close with his ear to the door, he heard the footsteps nearing and then stop but could not tell if they were directly outside or one door away. He was "sweating bullets," as he later told Ingolf, until he heard the jingle of keys followed by the sound of metal scraping against metal. It was just next door! Gunnar went limp with relief, and it took a few moments to catch his breath and pull himself together. He put the radio in the box, opened and closed the door softly behind him, and tiptoed down the hall to the back stairs. His heart was still pounding when he hid the box in a seldom-used basement storage area. It would be safe there until he was ready to take the bus home. Back in the lobby, he returned the master key to its hook and went outside. He stood for some time on the sidewalk taking deep breaths.

When Gunnar reached the bus terminal with the box under his arm, he began to worry about one more hurdle in getting home.

Placards had recently been posted in trams and buses warning that anyone refusing to sit next to a German soldier or uniformed Hird party member would be put off at the next stop and could be subject to a fine or punishment. This order was in response to the *is-fronten* (cold shoulder) campaign that the Norwegians engaged in to show their true feelings about the Quislings and the occupying Germans. Furthermore, any suspicious looking person and their belongings had also been subject to search ever since the Germans arrived.

Gunnar was growing nervous at the thought of having to take an empty seat next to a German or Hird member and possibly being asked what was in the box. It would do little good to pretend not to understand German or poorly spoken Norwegian, an excuse many people used, if he was faced with a finger pointing unmistakably at the box. He came up with the idea of saying it was a gift-wrapped present for his mother's birthday, if challenged; maybe they would be reluctant to mess up the packaging. His paranoia was beginning to take other imaginative flights when the bus pulled up. He need not have worried: there were no soldiers, police, or uniformed Hird on board and none got on before he reached his stop at Hinna.

Shortly after Ivar and Mathilde moved into the house, they had enlarged the kitchen by flooring over steps in the back entrance corner and enclosing the area. Now, with Gunnar's help Ivar cut a three-by-two foot section out of the new flooring. They kept the radio hidden on one of the old steps and covered the new trap door with a rug. Since the foundation did not extend under the old stair section, a search of the basement would not indicate a secret hiding area.

As cold waters to a thirsty soul, so is good news
from a far country.
Proverbs 25:25

Once again they could listen to the BBC's 7:30 p.m. Norwegian Service. A few minutes before each broadcast, Ivar would pull back the rug, lift the floor section, and lower Gunnar down to pick up the set. They always posted a lookout and Ivar made sure his few trusted friends came at staggered times so as not to alert any police or possible informers. Gunnar, of course, never mentioned the radio to any of his playmates or passed on any news that might give it away.

The day after taking the radio, Gunnar felt a knot in his stomach all the way to work. He was worried that the theft would cause an uproar. After he put on his uniform and went up to the lobby, the front desk clerk called him over to tell him that the assistant manager wanted to see him. With a sinking feeling, Gunnar went down the hall and knocked at the side of the opened door. The feeling doubled as he entered and saw the assistant manager and the housekeeper standing to one side, and sitting behind the desk a very intimidating Gestapo officer with jagged silver Old Norse runes on his gray uniform lapels. Most Gestapo switched to gray after 1939.

The assistant manager asked Gunnar if he knew or had heard anything about a radio that was missing from one of the third floor rooms. Though weak in the knees, Gunnar said he had not, doing his best to look surprised and innocent. The German looked on sternly without saying a word. Gunnar was not sure they were convinced, but after a few moments the German jerked his head slightly towards the door and the assistant manager told Gunnar he could go. Later he heard that several other employees had also been questioned, but like Gunnar they were relatively new to the staff. He also learned that the radio's owner had just returned the evening before after being away a week, so it was impossible to tell when the theft had taken place. Gunnar thought this might have been a factor in their decision not to pursue an investigation. But he also noticed that the master key was no longer on its usual hook. He decided to be very careful from then on.

Ivar had not had the radio for very long when a strange phenomenon occurred. The Høynes telephone was on a party line with one other neighbor, and callers to both houses began to hear Radio Norway broadcasts in the background when the phone was answered. Since only members of the military and the Quisling party could legally have radios, the Høynes family had an awkward time explaining the interference until it suddenly stopped for no apparent reason.

It was around this time that the Høynes family had a surprise visit from the Isaksens, along with their daughter-in-law Janna and grandson Johnny, now five years old. They had come from Skudenes to see relatives and wanted to hear if Ivar had any news from his friend Josef Isaksen in America. Mathilde and Marion were particularly interested in hearing about Janna's time in the Grini prison camp. Janna told them she was given a number and all possessions taken. She had a heartwarming story. One morning, Janna and the other women had been forced to strip naked and stand in formation in front of the guards. Janna looked around at what seemed to her a ridiculous scene and started to laugh. Quickly laughter spread through the ranks until nearly all the women were doubled over in hysterics. The German guards were infuriated. They could not understand why the women were laughing. Their prurient attempt to humiliate and intimidate the women had completely backfired. A simple act by one indomitable woman had brought so much comfort to her fellow prisoners.

17

THE RUSSIAN PRISONERS

I was in prison, and ye came unto me.

Matthew 25:36

onths later when winter was setting in, Gunnar was on an errand outside the hotel when he stopped to watch some horse–drawn wagons go by carrying German soldiers. They were followed by a guarded column of Russian prisoners of war. It was a cold day and the Germans wore heavy, long winter coats, but the prisoners—there must have been nearly fifty on the work detail—wore nothing more than flimsy, threadbare uniforms with vertical black stripes. Some had rags wrapped around their feet instead of shoes and all were gaunt and emaciated. Gunnar could scarcely believe his eyes when several prisoners stooped down and grabbed balls of horse manure to eat. Others snatched up bits of turf from the edges of the road to chew on.

When he got home that evening Gunnar talked about it with his parents and family. Ingolf had actually seen the new Russian prisoner camp and workshops down by the water in the adjacent village of Vaulen. He had heard that in addition to work on the roads and fortifications around Stavanger, prisoners made nails and boxed material and supplies for shipment to other parts of Norway. Most of the family had seen prison details from Poland and occasionally France, but none were treated as badly as the Russians. Gunnar had trouble falling asleep that night thinking about them. He wondered if there was a way he could help.

On a day off, Gunnar walked over to where Ingolf said the camp was located to see what it was like. It encompassed about two acres, bordered on one side by the fjord. The land portion was enclosed by two barbed wire fences about ten feet apart and eight feet high. There were the usual "Achtung" signs every hundred feet or so warning everyone to stay away or risk being shot. Clustered at one end of the compound were one-story wooden barracks, raised about two feet on cinder blocks. In the middle, a parade ground muster area separated the barracks from two large warehouse-like sheds where the work was done. On each of the two inland corners was a guard tower with a searchlight manned by a single soldier with a machine gun. The fjord side had only one barbed wire fence about six feet in from shore. It was not a highly secure arrangement; even if a prisoner was able to escape the compound, the Germans did not expect a shaved-head skeleton in a striped prison uniform to get very far.

Gunnar stayed well out of sight of the guard towers while he examined the layout and how it was guarded. He returned that night after dark to see what the lighting was like and whether the guard schedule and routes were the same. In addition to the guards in the watchtowers, two guards on foot with rifles patrolled inside the perimeter. They would meet at the center opposite the main gate and talk a bit before turning back along the fence to the water. Gunnar timed their round to average nine minutes. Getting in seemed almost impossible, but the fact that the single fence along the water was not patrolled gave him something to consider. He gave it a great deal of thought for the next several days and finally decided to go ahead with his plan after one more visit. He needed to know how deep the water was and the approximate angle of the slope to shore. Gunnar took Rex along, and staying well away from the fence, threw some sticks out. He rolled up his pants and followed Rex in to the water. The bottom was sandy and surprisingly gradual but the water was cold. Looking over, he noticed the guard in the tower staring at him, probably wondering what kind of game the boy was playing.

After his parents had gone to bed, Gunnar tiptoed down to the kitchen and took a few more slices of bread to add to the cache he had been accumulating for several days in a tin in the basement along with a small bag of tobacco. He wrapped everything in a scarf that he tied around his neck, pocketed a wire cutter and flashlight, and headed out. Twenty minutes later he waded into the fjord about fifty yards away from the prison compound. He went out up to his knees and, crouching over, slowly made his way toward the camp. Dim lights shone from the shaded perimeter lamps and there was the occasional sweeping beam of a tower searchlight. As he moved closer, Gunnar felt reasonably safe because of his low profile and distance from shore. Twenty feet past the corner of the compound, where one of the barracks shielded him from the searchlights, he headed in. On shore, he lay prone until he saw a guard reach the corner, look down the waterside fence, and turn back. Gunnar shielded the flashlight for a quick look at his watch. He crawled to the fence and was relieved to find that it was not buried like the other sides. He was able to squirm under it and reach the side of the building while staying in the shadow. After the searchlight passed, he crouched down and hurried around the corner to a door, which pushed open easily. The smell inside was intolerable. There was little light except what dimly came through the dirty windows and brightened for a few seconds when the searchlight made its periodic sweep.

Gunnar was quickly surrounded by ghostlike figures. Their incredulous, wide, sunken eyes were frightening. They seemed to lack focus; he had not realized that the prisoners' meager no-fat diet caused night blindness. Gunnar undid the bundle from his neck, opened it, and took out the pieces of bread. He broke off bits to place in the emaciated claws that stretched forth. There must have been a dozen of these creatures pressed around him in the darkness. They hardly made a sound until he held out the tobacco in the palm of his hand and put a pinch in each of theirs. Some mumbled a few words he did not understand, then one stepped forward holding out something that Gunnar had trouble recognizing at first. A sweep of light passed the window, and he saw that it was a handful of nails from the workshop: a gift. Gunnar shook his head. If he was caught by the Germans with anything showing he had contact with prisoners or stolen any military supplies, he could be shot on the spot. The Russian prisoners, on the other hand, could not understand how this thirteen-year-old Norwegian boy had been able to sneak past the German guards—and why he would risk his life to bring them bread and tobacco.

Gunnar was not certain that he could come back, but seeing the gratitude on the prisoners' faces, he let them know in halting German that he would try. Checking his watch with the shielded flashlight, he slipped out the door and around to the shadowed side of the building. He rolled up his trousers and, teeth chattering from the cold, crawled back under the fence to the water. Gunnar retraced his earlier route, and once ashore put on the socks and shoes he had hidden in a bush. With warm feet, shoes on, and a tremendous sense of accomplishment, he ran like the wind. It was not only a relief to be safe and heading home but deep down Gunnar felt an emotional upheaval. He had brought a little solace and perhaps a little hope to human beings who had virtually none. His child's world had changed the day Norway was invaded and now he had the opportunity and sense of purpose to defy the Germans.

Mathilde used to warn the children that telling a lie would turn their tongues black, which she could see but they could not, and Gunnar thought of this as he got in bed. The next morning he tried to explain to Mor the wet, muddy clothes she had spotted in the back hall before he got up. She did not believe his story of falling off a rock while night fishing. She was also aware of the missing pieces of bread. This all tied in with the intensity he had shown recently talking about the Russian prisoners. It was becoming a tired refrain, but once again she could only say, "Please be more careful."

Gunnar made several more trips to the prison and finally did accept a few small handcarved figurines from the Russians. His last visit was a close call. One evening, after the beam of the searchlight passed the barracks and he had slipped out the door and rounded the corner, the searchlight unexpectedly flashed back. It stopped for several seconds before continuing its sweep. Gunnar knew the guards had spotted something. In the building's shadow, he ran to the fence, crawled under, and headed out into the water. Fortunately, he had a good start before he heard the sound of boots running. He looked back to see the silhouette of two guards rounding the corner of the building. Crouching low over the water and inching along, Gunnar looked back again and saw the guards walking the fence line and shining their flashlights on the ground. Their voices rose, and he knew they had discovered the marks where he crawled under the fence. They flashed their lights out on the water. Gunnar was already past the compound and heading into shore as fast as he dared without splashing. He was skirting the compound on his way home when he saw extra lights come on and heard the shouts of guards rousting prisoners for roll call. Back home in the basement, he shivered so uncontrollably that he hardly had the strength to strip off his soaked clothing. He never went back, certain the Germans would have increased security on the water side of the camp.

At war's end there were over eighty thousand Russian prisoners of war in Norway. Under army jurisdiction there, they had fared a little better, but not much, than in countries where special SS units ran the concentration and death camps. Russia's leader, Stalin, demanded all prisoners be returned, even those requesting asylum or found in hiding months and years later. Tragically, almost all were either worked to death in the gulag prisons or executed, even the women nurses. Exposure to the living standards and ideas of the West or surrender under any conditions were almost certain death sentences.

After the German defeat at Stalingrad, German soldiers who were sent to Russia knew they were being sent to their graves. Gunnar could see it in the faces of men boarding the transports docked in the ship basin next to the hotel. Whenever he heard one of the military bands strike up a stirring march, he ducked out of the hotel for a quick look. It was usually a sendoff to the eastern front, and no one was smiling. Russia's retribution to Germany and the German people for their atrocities would be terrible and the Germans knew it.

18

OUTFOXING THE GERMANS

Action is eloquence.

Shakespeare, *Coriolanus*

akob was anxious to get home and join Milorg, the organized resistance, along with his best friend, Peter Skrettingland. Shortly after his nineteenth birthday he was formally inducted and given a brief training in the use of firearms and security measures. His three-person team, which included Peter, was directed by a member of Milorg who was known only to one of them. In case any of the group was captured and tortured, there would be the least danger to the organization. In addition, the only information passed along was strictly limited by a "need to know" regulation.

The main assignment for Jakob's team was to deliver machine guns and arms throughout the Stavanger area that had been smuggled in from the British Isles. Most weapons were landed further up the coast by the "Shetland Bus" group of Norwegian fishing boat skippers. Throughout the war, they took their small sixty- and seventy-foot one-cylinder "puffers" on three and four day journeys through some of the most treacherous seas in the world. They brought agents and supplies to Norway and returned to their Shetland Island base with refugees and rescued Allied airmen. Jakob would be told where to pick up guns, and at night he redelivered them to various locations. The boathouse was one hiding place, but Mathilde did not appreciate finding a machine gun under her sofa when cleaning one day.

Jakob had a narrow escape early one morning when returning on his bike from a night delivery. He was in a rural area with narrow roads and little traffic at that hour. But as he rounded a curve, he came face to face with a German soldier and a uniformed woman, walking side by side and blocking his path. They made no attempt to get out of his way, and Jakob stopped. Tired and irritable, he told them in no uncertain terms to move aside. The German took a swing at Jakob and missed. Letting go of the bike, Jakob knocked him back into a drainage ditch. The woman nurse or clerk—he was not sure which—began yelling at Jakob. He was about to push her into the ditch also when he spotted out of the corner of his eye a truck full of soldiers coming around the bend. Thinking quickly, Jakob jumped down into the ditch, helped the soldier to his feet, and let him flail away while the truck passed. The dozen soldiers in back laughed at the sight of a Norwegian being beaten up. Jakob protected his face with his forearms, and when the truck was out of sight he immediately pushed the German back down. As Jakob biked away, the woman screamed something at him in German that did not sound very ladylike. He turned and blew her a kiss.

The next day Jakob ran into some buddies downtown. They told him that a German soldier with a black eye accompanied by a policeman had been stopping at various cafés looking for someone who fit Jakob's description. He laid low for a few days but could not say anything about it at home. Of course, Gunnar and Ingolf were dying to know details and hinted continuously at wanting to know why he was staying home and out of sight. Jakob wouldn't bite but did share some of the chocolate he got from Milorg, the usual reward along with a few cigarettes after a mission.

> *It is by losing himself in the objective, in inquiry,*
> *creation, and craft, that a man becomes something.*
> Paul Goodman, *The Community of Scholars*

One evening after leaving work at the hotel, Gunnar noticed a German tank parked close to a barracks along the bus route. He thought little about it at the time, but it was still there a week later and the partially opened hatch propped up for ventilation was inviting. Every time the bus passed it the next few days, Gunnar thought about ways of getting inside to see what he could find. It was not promising. There was never a guard nearby, but the tank was only about twenty feet from the building and soldiers living there could often be seen looking out a nearby window.

Finally one night Gunnar decided to take a look and quietly sneaked out of the house. To avoid curfew patrols, he wended his way through backyards and side streets until he was across the street from the barracks, hidden behind a large bush. It had taken him almost half an hour, but he had the patience to stay out of sight for another ten minutes to make sure there was no guard or night patrol. The moon was full, but a procession of low-flying clouds cast occasional shadows, and he darted across in one. He crouched next to the tank's treads on the side away from the barracks and examined the tank for hand or foot holds. Once he found the first handgrip, it was easy going, and he cautiously climbed up.

Near the partly opened hatch he started to have second thoughts. Although the Germans were ruthless about enforcing blackout restrictions, particularly along the coast, they were often sloppy themselves, and one of the windows directly opposite the tank was half open with the shade up. It was a hot summer night with almost no breeze, and Gunnar could clearly hear soldiers talking and laughing through the opened window. He realized that if they looked out and saw him in the light, he could probably jump down and start running, but could not escape. German soldiers did not hesitate to shoot for any reason and he would not have time to get back across the wide road.

After agonizing for a moment, Gunnar stood up on the last foothold and pushed the hatch fully back. He gripped the rim and lowered himself down feet first. At shoulder level he let go to drop down what he hoped was no more than a foot to the floor. He only went a few inches before his feet slid out from under him. A resounding series of metallic clangs reverberated inside the tank. He had landed on a pile of empty brass shell casings, which rolled off in all directions. Gunnar's ears were ringing and his heart nearly stopped. The Germans surely must have heard the loud clash of metal against metal. He dared not move a muscle or breathe for almost a minute. Then he stood up very slowly so as not to disturb any more casings. Through the open hatch, he could hear the Germans still talking and laughing, sounds he never believed he would find so comforting.

Gunnar waited a few more moments to catch his breath and let his eyes adjust to the dark interior. Looking around he saw a machine gun on the floor, two metal boxes that looked like ammunition, and a narrow ladder leading up to the hatch, which he had missed while getting in. He climbed up with one ammunition box and set it on a flat section of the turret before going back down to wrestle with the machine gun. Fortunately it had a carrying strap, but it was a lot heavier than he had anticipated. Also, the bipod rest near the end of the barrel wanted to snag on every corner as he pulled the gun up and over the hatch opening. He was sweating through his shirt by the time he got everything on the ground and dashed across the road under another cloud's shadow.

Getting home took twice as long. Gunnar felt as if his arms were being pulled out of his shoulder sockets by the heavy gun, and he had to stop and rest every few minutes. He also had to stay close to bushes and walls for cover in case of a patrol or stray soldier. It was near midnight when Gunnar reached the house and stashed everything away in the cellar. He hid the machine gun in a long wooden storage box with some old tools on the lid. Halfway up the stairs in his stocking feet, he heard Mor's voice in the shadow of her bedroom door. "Gunnar, where have you been? I checked your bed an hour ago and was just about to wake your father. I was really worried." It was perhaps only the second time in his life that he lied to his mother, but all he could think to say was that he had forgotten to do something at the hotel and had to go back. Mor clearly was not convinced but said only, "Please get to bed." When Gunnar came down to brush his teeth in the morning, the first thing he did was look in the mirror and stick out his tongue.

Every day the following week Gunnar peeked at his trophy, and when his mother was away shopping one morning, he decided to give it a test. First, he figured out how to feed in the ammunition belt. Then with a shell in the chamber, he snapped the lid down and released the safety. He lined up several thick boards against the wall and set the bipod to rest on a box. Aiming carefully, he pulled the trigger. There was only a click and dead silence. Gunnar unloaded the belt and shells and with the chamber open, pulled the trigger. Nothing appeared from the small hole on the face of the bolt. The firing pin had been removed. Gunnar never was the least discouraged when confronted with a mechanical problem, and his innate curiosity about machinery immediately took charge. He grabbed a rule and calipers and started measuring.

Whenever he had a spare moment in the next few weeks, Gunnar retreated to the workbench. Using a hacksaw, files, and emery cloth, he slowly machined a new pin. It was a lengthy process of trial and error, but he finally got the pin to fit and shoot forward smoothly when he pulled the trigger. He waited several days until he was off work and his mother had gone shopping. Once again, he set up planks against the wall, loaded the belt, and rested the barrel on a tall box. Releasing the safety, Gunnar pulled the trigger. There was a tremendous jolt. His shoulder felt like it had been kicked by a mule and, still firing, the gun's barrel swung violently up and around. His index finger was jammed between the trigger and trigger guard. Only three or four seconds of firing passed before he could get his hand away, but about seventy rounds had been sprayed all around the cellar. The M-36 machine gun could fire almost nine hundred rounds per minute. Gunnar sat in a daze with his bruised shoulder, a sprained finger, ears ringing, and eyes watering. He was still shaking a half-hour later when he put everything back in the wooden box. He opened the outside door to fan out the smell of gunpowder before taking a long walk to clear his head and settle his nerves.

At supper that evening, Far mentioned that a neighbor had heard the Germans doing a lot of shooting nearby. He asked if anyone knew anything about it. There was dead silence. Gunnar looked down at his plate and poked at a rutabaga. Out of the corner of his eye, he saw Mor turn toward him with an inquiring look. Four-year-old Anna looked back and forth between her mother and adored older brother, wondering what was going on. For the next several days, Gunnar was a most dutiful son, telling his mother, "Please Mor, let me get it for you" whenever she headed toward the basement door. Mor was not born yesterday, however.

19

THE GESTAPO

Freedom is when one hears the bell at

seven o'clock in the morning and knows it is the

milkman and not the Gestapo.

Georges Bidault, French resistance leader and Prime Minister

Gunnar was determined to avoid any trouble at work after the radio incident. He was not particularly concerned when he arrived at the hotel one morning and learned that a pistol had been stolen sometime the day before. Usually when the manager or his assistant needed Gunnar for an errand, the desk clerk said, "Gunnar, the manager needs you." This time, however, he said, "Gunnar, you'd better see the manager right away." Gunnar felt his internal alarm bell start to ring. It was about the missing pistol, and Gunnar was told to go over to the Gestapo headquarters immediately and report to a certain major. The assistant manager looked at Gunnar sympathetically. "Now, don't worry," he said. "You're not the only one they want to talk to."

The headquarters was about a fifteen minute walk through the center of town and up the hill toward Eiganes. The building's surrounding streets were cordoned off with cement pylon barricades and armed guards. Inside the building entrance, Gunnar gave his name and the name of the officer he was supposed to see to a soldier at the desk. The soldier picked up a phone, spoke briefly, then hung up and told Gunnar to follow him. They walked past several rows of people working at desks then down a corridor. The soldier stopped at one of the opened doors and gestured for Gunnar to enter. It was a large office with an imposing desk and a very stern looking officer sitting behind it. He beckoned Gunnar to step forward and then, scowling, asked him what his duties were at the hotel and whether he know anything about a pistol that was missing. Gunnar truthfully said he did not, throwing in a lot of "yes sirs" and "no sirs."

Finally the officer stood up and paced back and forth for a few moments. He stopped abruptly and, turning to Gunnar, asked, "What if we search your house?" The German appeared to have grown about ten feet tall. Gunnar's heart was in his mouth. In his basement were a machine gun, three pistols, ammunition, and a few grenades thrown in for good measure. His entire family would go to prison or worse if the Germans found out. Without hesitation, Gunnar responded, "You can go ahead. We have nothing to hide."

The Gestapo officer looked hard at Gunnar for what seemed like ages before telling him to wait outside in the hall. Gunnar stayed close enough to hear the officer make a phone call, but he could not hear what was being said. After a few minutes he was ordered back in and brusquely told to go back to work. While returning to the hotel, Gunnar wondered if they might search the house, and he began to worry about his mother. He ducked inside the back entrance, changed out of his uniform, and waited for a few minutes before leaving. Although he felt relatively inconspicuous in regular clothes, he stopped at several different places in town as though still running errands. He did not think he was being followed, but it was just like the Gestapo to check up on him. Finally, he jumped in a taxi at a stand near the hotel and headed out to Hinna.

Two blocks from home, Gunnar spotted an unfamiliar black Fiat sedan parked near his house. It had no converter tank, which meant it belonged to the police or military. Quickly, he had the taxi turn down a side street and stop where he would be out of sight.

He raced through several backyards to his house and slipped in the rear cellar entrance to sit and wait. There was nothing he could do at this late hour to hide all the weapons, but he wanted to be near Mor if the Germans came. Sitting quietly on a box, he could hear Mor's unmistakable shuffling around the kitchen in her slippers. He sat for about thirty minutes before opening the cellar door. At the corner of the house, he peeked through one of the ornamental bushes. The car was gone!

Gunnar did not want to disturb his mother, and having been away from work for almost two hours, he headed straight back to town on the bus. The desk clerk was starting to be concerned when he showed up. Gunnar explained that the Gestapo major had been called away on something important and they had made him wait but were not charging him with anything. The next day at work, Gunnar still felt a little wrung out from his first encounter with the Gestapo. He felt awfully lucky, though, to have seen what was certainly a surveillance team before they saw him. Midmorning, his sense of relief was shattered when he was called back to Gestapo headquarters. "Now I've had it!" he thought. The Gestapo never needed proof. People were tortured and executed on mere suspicion. The Gestapo police were accountable to no one but Hitler and people arrested usually just disappeared and were never heard from again.

Gunnar was led to the same office and told to go in. The major looked even larger and more sinister. Gunnar could feel his knees shaking but tried to keep an innocent, inquiring look on his face. The German glared at him for what again seemed like ages before demanding, "Have you ever thought of stealing anything?" Without blinking an eye, Gunnar replied, "Yes, and it would be very easy to do but I didn't take the pistol you're looking for." The officer stared at him for a moment and then looked up at the ceiling. He reached across the desk to pick up a folder and without looking at Gunnar said matter-of-factly, "You can go." Gunnar could hardly believe his ears: strangely enough, that was the end of it. As he left the feared building, it felt exceptionally wonderful to drink in the fresh air and see the free-flying gulls.

> *Beware of all enterprises that require new clothes.*
> Henry D. Thoreau

Feeling awfully good a few days later, Gunnar decided to splurge and use up his savings on a new suit. He was always neat and particular about his appearance, but he was also developing an interest in girls and there was one in particular he wanted to impress. On his day off, he went to the store in Hinna and picked out a navy blue suit from the very limited supply. The fit was reasonably close, and he was told to stop by in a few days to pick it up. After trying it on to check the tailoring, he decided to wear it home and go past the girl's house. Halfway home, he got caught in a sudden downpour and was thoroughly soaked. He ran the last few blocks. Something started to feel different about the suit but he was hardly prepared for the reception he got from the family. First there were astonished looks, then giggles from Marion, and snickers from Ingolf. The wartime synthetic fabric, heavily laden with cellulose, had stretched dramatically in the rain and the suit seemed to have doubled in size. Gunnar was terribly let down having used up almost all his savings and coupons. When four-year-old Anna burst out laughing, Gunnar could not help from joining her. Then everyone started. He never wore the suit again.

Fortune assists the brave.
Terence, *Phormio*

One evening, Jakob was having a cup of ersatz (fake) coffee with a friend upstairs in one of the cafes when a slightly wobbly and nervous-looking German soldier appeared in the doorway. The soldier stood for a few moments surveying the room and the people seated at the tables. He had the look and mannerisms of someone on his way to the eastern front, Jakob later recalled. Then he made eye contact with Jakob, who had not lowered his head like most everyone. He glared at Jakob before striding over and grabbing him by the shirt as if to say, "Don't you dare look at me that way." But before the German could say a word, Jakob stood up and flattened him with one punch. A hush descended over the crowd as the soldier slowly struggled to get up, holding his jaw.

Just as Jakob turned to tell his friend they better leave, three leather-jacketed Gestapo secret police he had not noticed before jumped up from a far corner table. They charged across the room, and chairs were knocked aside as customers tried to get out of the way. Jakob was grabbed before he could escape. Two held his arms, while the other hammered away with both fists at his face, midsection, and groin. After a dozen blows, they threw him on the floor. Jakob lay in a fetal position while all three participated in kicking him. They dragged him out the door onto the stair landing, then picked him up and tossed him over the railing into the side yard. Jakob lay listlessly while the Germans watched for a few moments, debating whether to go down and check his condition. Finally they turned and left; either they assumed he was near death or thought he had been taught enough of a lesson. Jakob's friend, who had stayed in the distance, went down to see what damage had been done.

It took a while for Jakob to get up and move, but he did not appear to have any broken bones. Miraculously, he was just bloody and badly bruised. His friend helped him stay upright as they slowly made their way to a taxi stand. Gunnar heard the soft knock at the door first, and the minute he opened it he called for his mother. Mor, hearing the urgency in Gunnar's voice, raced in from the kitchen. She hardly recognized the red swollen face in front of her. Gunnar and the friend helped Jakob to a chair while Mathilde called Ivar to come from the study and help. The friend said only, "He's lucky to be alive at all," and quickly left. Mathilde kept asking what had happened but Jakob would not tell her. After a couple of days in bed and a visit from Dr. Høynes, Jakob was up and moving around gingerly but still not talking. Mathilde felt she was about to have a nervous breakdown not knowing what to expect next from the three boys. As the war drew to a close, Mathilde was nearly distraught as the

Germans became more desperate and vengeful.

After the 1944 Allied landings in Normandy, the Germans, fearful of an impending uprising by the underground, intensified their household searches for arms. Summary on-the-spot executions were common for those caught, so Mathilde decided she had better act. She told Gunnar that if there was anything in the house that might be a "problem," he should get rid of it for the family's sake. He felt quite ashamed when he realized what a terrible risk he had taken and said only, "Yes, Mor." That night, he went to the basement and made sure all the weapons and ammunition were packed together in the wood box. He drilled several holes in the sides and added a few rocks for good measure. Later, around two o'clock in the morning, Gunnar rose, dressed, and lugged the crate out the back basement entrance and across the road to the communal dock. It was much heavier than he had realized and he had to set it down and rest several times. Finally he got it out to the end of the dock and heaved it over. He waited while it slowly disappeared. On the way home, he still felt quite guilty at the thought of what the Germans would have done to the family had they ever searched his home.

> *The price of pride is high and is paid by the young.*
> German War Memorial at El Alamein

A few days later Jakob came home with a gruesome story of what to expect from the Germans. He had seen the body of a German sailor hanged by the neck from a tree near the massive concrete submarine pens. Pinned to the corpse's chest was a placard with the notice that this was punishment for cowards who refuse to continue on submarine missions for "The Fuhrer and Fatherland." The grisly display remained for almost a week. It was common knowledge around Stavanger that submariners were the most nervous and unpredictable members of the occupying forces, after being cooped up for months in potential coffins. Even their countrymen in other military branches gave them a wide berth.

LIBERATION

Oh courage...oh yes! If only one had that...Then life

might be livable, in spite of everything.

Ibsen, *Hedda Gabler*

he winter of 1944-45 was the worst of the entire war. The potato harvest had failed and there were record cold spells. In November, the German 20th Mountain Army retreated from Finland into Norway's most northern district, Finnmark, and under orders from Berlin began one of the worst scorched earth operations in the war. Finnmark was Norway's most sparsely populated county with only about 48,000 people in 50,000 square miles. Everyone was ordered to leave and head south with only the belongings they could carry. All homes were razed or burned, cattle destroyed, and 80,000 mines planted. Those who hid were executed if discovered. As refugees streamed south, the rest of the country became aware of the extent of the catastrophe. It was a foretaste of a possible "Fortress Norway" blood-

Jakob (top row, far right) with Milorg team
Photograph by Henry Meldahl for the Stavanger Aftenblad

bath ending to the war. Rumors of a last stand in Norway had been circulating with some validity. The Germans had almost 400,000 well-equipped troops there in strong defensive positions under one of their most capable and ruthless generals.

News of Hitler's suicide in the Berlin bunker on April 30 swept around the world. Everyone knew the war in Europe would be over shortly—except the Norwegians. They were held in a state of suspense until the last minute, when at 10:15 p.m. on May 7, 1945, the commanding German, General Boehme, called on his soldiers in a radio address to surrender peacefully and to conduct themselves honorably in the best tradition of the German Army. It was the last occupied country that the Germans surrendered, and Boehme had been prepared to fight on if given the command. Fortunately he was not, and the Germans laid down their arms without incident, due in no small part to the exemplary behavior and discipline of Milorg, the Norwegian armed resistance.

The day following Boehme's announcement, Jakob was in a small group of twelve Milorg members assigned to take over the Gestapo headquarters in Stavanger. His unit commandeered—actually, stole—a truck, and with their armbands and hats proclaiming their organizational identity they entered and took over the building. First, for their own safety they shot the vicious Alsatian dogs the Gestapo had used to track down and attack people. Then they rounded up all the Germans in the large entertainment room, which had a dance floor and grand piano. Some of the Milorg men stared in fascination at the marks on top of the piano made by the high heels of dancing girls. Only one German caused any trouble. A particularly nasty-looking captain started mouthing off but quickly stopped when Jakob jammed a pistol in his ear and told him to shut up.

All day long while the Germans were stacking arms and being rounded up in groups for transport back to Germany, Norwegians were congregating to celebrate. Hidden Bibles and family treasures were dug up or taken out of secret places. Every available Norwegian flag was displayed. Candles were lit in every window, and in Hinna the national anthem blared forth from an open window in the Høines family house—"Ja, Vi Elsker Dette Landet" ("Yes, We

Love This Land"). It came from the only radio in the neighborhood. Fourteen-year-old Gunnar was especially proud that the radio had been made in Norway, not Germany, and that it had not been stolen, only rightfully taken back.

In downtown Stavanger, six-year-old Anna was separated from her mother in the crowd but was soon joyfully reunited. Ten-year-old Nils rowed over with a friend from Roaldsøy to the now-abandoned fort on the adjacent island. Everywhere, the Germans had simply walked away, leaving explosives, equipment, and arms lying about. Nils and his buddy gathered a good supply of dynamite and had marvelous fishing for the next several months.

At three o'clock, church bells rang steadily for a full hour throughout the land. Most had been cast from iron, a less precious metal than the old bronze ones, but that day they sounded like they were made of pure gold.

Epilogue

t the end of the war, Mr. Lund tried to convince Gunnar to make a career of the hotel business, but America beckoned. At nineteen he shook hands with his mother at the dock opposite the Victoria Hotel and boarded the SS *Stavangerfjord* for the United States. There he started work as a fisherman in Massachusetts with the Isaksen friends of his father. He married his boss's daughter, Eleanor, and together they had four children. Gunnar left fishing in New Bedford for the offshore oil industry in California, and before retiring he captained ships that serviced oil rigs throughout the world. Prior to his death in October 2002, his daughter, Susan Mechler, had taken notes and recorded some of his experiences during the occupation. A typical Norwegian, he did not think anyone would be interested.

Eleanor, Gunnar's widow, lives in the Massachusetts home he so loved overlooking Buzzards Bay. Anna, married to Henry Vigre, and Ingolf, a widower, live in Stavanger. Jakob was a member of the King's Guard before emigrating to the United States in 1952. He anglicized his name to Jack Haines and made ship models for the Stevens Institute in Hoboken, New Jersey. He then went to Alaska where he and a Swedish partner were newsworthy as the last commercial fishermen to use an open boat with only a sail and oars for power. Subsequently, he designed and built houses on Long Island, New York where he retired with his wife, Gayle, who after a career in education helps preserve our maritime heritage with a focus on lighthouses.

Just before the war's end, Ingolf joined Milorg and subsequently served in Germany with the Tysklands Brigaden where he received the King's Order of Merit. Mathilde died in 1977 and Ivar four years later in 1981. Janna Isaksen died in 2005 in a Massachusetts nursing home. In her last days she had delusions about the nurses being Gestapo members. Nils Roaldsøy, now retired on Roaldsøy, the family's island, became a pilot and national hero with the Norwegian Air Force when he headed the North Sea helicopter rescue squadron. Marion died of a brain tumor in middle age. Mikal, Gunnar's grandfather, died at the age of ninety-three. Until nearly the end, he rowed across to Stavanger from Steinsøy several times a week and climbed the hill to visit Anna's grave next to the church with the tall white steeple.

Gunnar and Sigrid Gundersen frequently return to Norway from their home in Massachusetts. On a recent trip they visited a famous scenic overlook and overheard an elderly tourist tell his companion in German, "To think all of this could have been ours!"

A Brief History of Norway

efore the age of the Vikings, numerous petty kings ruled all of Scandinavia. Then around 900 A.D. Harold I drove out many of the nobles to Iceland and France, conquered the Shetland and Orkney islands north of Scotland, and ruled much of present-day Norway. After his death in 935, two sons fought for the throne and Haakon I prevailed. He was followed by Olaf I and Olaf II, "the Fat" (or more politely, "the Stout") who introduced Christianity but was later forced out by King Canute of Denmark with the help of discontented nobles. During this period, Scandinavian notables had some wonderfully descriptive names. Svein Forkbeard, Harald Bluetooth, Thorolf Lousebeard, Hrolf the Walker (so called because he was so big no horse could carry him), and a court poet, Eyvind the Plagiarist, are good examples.

Canute conquered Britain in 1013 A.D., and for the first time Sweden, Norway, and Denmark had a single ruler. His efforts to strengthen the Church were not so fruitful. Unhappy with the pace of Sweden's conversion, he sent monks from England who ended up living like oriental potentates. Many drank themselves to death and a certain Bishop Henry was said to "never have raised his hand in blessing unless there was a glass in it."

Canute was followed by Magnus I and then Harald Hardrada, who is best known for invading northern England in 1066 and being defeated at Stamford Bridge by Harold of England. Having staved off one Scandinavian threat, Harold force-marched a tired and depleted army 150 miles south to Hastings only to be vanquished and killed, ironically, by other Viking descendents from Normandy under William the Conqueror. Thereafter, Norway's fortunes declined until the twelfth century when there was a permanent migration of herring from the southern Baltic shores to Norwegian waters. The next century was notable for the Black Death, a plague that wiped out more than one-third of the population. Then in 1397 Norway, Sweden, and Denmark were once again united under Margaret of Denmark. For the next four hundred years Norway was ruled by Denmark, until it was ceded to Sweden in 1815 as a result of Napoleonic War treaties that penalized the Danes for siding with France. Although semi-independent, Norwegians chafed under Swedish dominance and finally gained complete independence in 1905 after an overwhelming vote in a plebiscite. Carl, son of Frederick VIII of Denmark, became King Haakon VII in the new nation and was joined by his consort Queen Maude, the daughter of Edward VII of England.

Norway is a constitutional monarchy governed by the Storting (parliament), which meets in Oslo, the capitol. The country has many historical firsts and an enviable record in humanitarian and social causes. In 1851 it was the first European nation to grant Jews citizenship. In 1865 capital punishment was effectively ended. Universal suffrage was instituted in 1898 and in 1907 women were granted the vote (earlier for municipal elections). Norwegian accomplishments in exploration are unsurpassed; arctic explorers Roald Amundsen and Fridtjof Nansen are prime examples. With the discovery of North Sea oil in the late 1960's, Norway vaulted from being one of the poorer European nations to one of the world's richest. It was cited in 2002 as the best nation to live in, according to a United Nations survey.

The Vikings

s early as the seventh century, the Vikings made incursions from Scandinavia into what is now Russia. In the tenth century, their presence in trade, colonization, and as recipients of tribute was felt from Baghdad in Persia all the way to Greenland in North America. They were not only fierce warriors but were the finest shipbuilders and seamen in the world. After 800 A.D. their beautiful ships were the scourge of coastal communities and monasteries throughout much of western Europe and the British Isles.

A typical ship plying the Atlantic and European waters was seventy-six feet long, seventeen feet at its widest point amidships, and higher at the prow and stern. It drew just three feet of water fully loaded and amidships had only a three-foot freeboard (the distance from the water to the top edge of the uppermost plank). The keel was a single fifty-seven-foot piece of oak timber, and planks below the waterline were tied to the frames (ribs) with spruce root lashings. This latter feature gave the ship great flexibility and seaworthiness. It was single-masted with a square sail, usually with vertical stripes. The square sail gave the ship a helpful lift to take the bow up over a towering wave, versus a fore-and-aft rig (sloop, lateen, or schooner) that drives the bow into waves and uses the buoyancy of the hull alone to raise it. A ship this size normally carried thirty oarsmen but could hold ninety men. It was able to come in from the sea through shallow water to beach and quickly unload warriors, and the Vikings surprised and overran settlements and departed with valuables and captives before alarms could generate resistance. Few inhabitants were spared.

Not all Vikings were raiders. In the east, Vikings from Sweden, called Varangians, were founders of modern Russia. Settlements at Novgorod and Kiev controlled the Dnieper River down to the Black Sea and trade as far as Constantinople (now Istanbul, Turkey). They used the Volga River to carry fur and slaves from northern Russia to the Caspian Sea and then portage them across to Baghdad. The ships using routes requiring portage were of a special design—generally only forty feet long and with planks little more than half an inch thick to keep weight low. They were raised on beams with large wooden wheels and pulled by the crew and slaves overland. Portages of ten miles or more were not unusual.

In the western world, the Vikings settled Iceland in 770 A.D., Dublin in 841, and in France controlled at one time Cologne, Bordeaux, Orleans, and Rouen as well as all of Normandy. They reached Greenland in 982 and Nova Scotia, in North America, around 1000. They roamed the Mediterranean almost at will, established the Kingdom of Sicily, and controlled most of southern Italy. Seldom pointed out is their civilizing respect for the rule of law. Ironically, of the Great Powers only Germany escaped their influence in this regard. Never in history has such a small group in such a short period had so much impact on the course of civilization.

Norway: Hitler's Downfall?

I n mid-December 1939, a naval engagement eight thousand miles away from Norway in the South Atlantic triggered a chain of events that led to the *Altmark* affair two months later and changed Hitler's mind about respecting Norway's neutrality.

The *Altmark,* disguised as a modern tanker, was the armed supply ship for the German pocket-battleship *Graf Spee.* This raider had been the scourge of Allied shipping off Africa and in the southern hemisphere since the war started. In December 1939 a British naval officer, Commodore Henry Harwood, one of the war's unsung heroes, correctly calculated that the *Graf Spee* would head for the heavy shipping lanes off Argentina although its position was last reported three thousand miles away. Harwood then laid out a brilliant strategy of splitting his force of one 8-inch armed heavy cruiser and two light cruisers with 6-inch guns in order to divert the pocket-battleship's ability to concentrate its 11-inch gunfire. In one of the war's critical encounters, Britain's three-cruiser squadron crossed paths with the *Graf Spee* at dawn on December 13.

For over an hour, a fierce gunnery duel ensued. The *Graf Spee* put the heavy cruiser out of action and severely damaged the other two ships. But surprisingly, she broke off fighting and headed into Montevideo, Uruguay for repairs. She was not badly damaged, but her captain questioned her ability to survive North Atlantic winter conditions on the return to Germany. She was scuttled four days later in dramatic fashion rather than face what was assumed to be a greatly reinforced British squadron. In fact, reinforcements had not arrived; the Germans had been fooled by British propaganda. Hitler was furious that his ship had not gone down fighting. The British then began a frantic search for the *Altmark* loaded with seamen prisoners.

The *Altmark* eluded detection by staying south for two months before heading north beyond Iceland and the Arctic Circle. From there it sailed east to the protection of the neutral Norwegian coast, but was spotted by a British reconnaissance plane near Stavanger. A British destroyer was dispatched, and on February 16, 1940 it forced its way past two escorting Norwegian gunboats to close on the *Altmark,* which had ducked into the Jossingfjord. A boarding party freed 299 prisoners with little resistance from the Germans, who fled across ice to shore, losing six men. A British nation that had little to celebrate was ecstatic. Norwegians were embarrassed. Hitler was outraged. The Norwegian navy's failure to fight convinced him that Norway would not resist a rumored British invasion and he ordered his own invasion plan put into effect three days later.

Winston Churchill, as First Lord of the Admiralty, had already developed a keen interest in Norway. In December, Fritz Thyssen, a German industrialist who had a falling out with Hitler, told French intelligence that iron was in such short supply in Germany that stopping Swedish iron ore shipments coming through Norway during winter months "would bring Germany to its knees." Churchill promoted the idea of using the pretext of coming to Finland's aid against Russia as a way of conveniently cutting off Germany's main ore supply. He proposed landing at Narvik in northern Norway and crossing over to Finland, seizing the Swedish mines on the way. French and British units were embarking on ships for the operation when

Germany beat them to the punch.

The British-led counter-invasion in northern Norway was so mismanaged in comparison to German successes that a month later Prime Minister Neville Chamberlain was forced to resign. As a result, Winston Churchill took his place—and is generally credited as being the one individual most responsible for Hitler's defeat.

In the Norwegian campaign, Germany lost three cruisers, ten modern destroyers, a dozen supply ships, and suffered severe damage to other ships. Hitler refused to risk any more of his ships to stop the evacuation of trapped Allied troops at Dunkirk, France. Instead, he relied solely on the Luftwaffe there, and without any surface interference from the German navy, 335,000 British and French soldiers were saved. In one of history's most dramatic rescues, 860 ships ranging from ocean liners to cabin cruisers participated in the evacuation. Surrender at Dunkirk would have forced England to pull out of the war since Hitler was prepared to give very generous terms. After Dunkirk, German naval losses in Norway was one of the main reasons Hitler did not invade England, now virtually defenseless without heavy weapons.

British Commando raids in March and December of 1941 were initially puzzling to the Germans. Then an intelligence report by way of the Finnish embassy in Washington convinced Hitler that the raid on the strongly fortified island of Vaagso in December was a probing action for a much larger joint British-American operation in the spring. He immediately ordered a substantial increase in the number of troops in Norway and put a high priority on expanding and improving coastal defenses. A month later, Hitler ordered his reluctant admirals to concentrate all the navy's capital ships in Norway as well.

Hitler's obsession with Norway as the "Zone of Destiny" and

paranoia about Allied plans to return were the reasons he kept an unnecessarily large force there for the remainder of the war. Against repeated pleas from his generals, thirteen full-strength army divisions fortified Norway almost to the end. In his book *Vaagso Raid,* Joseph Devins, Jr. claims that more than half could have been spared and would have made a difference in Russia or Normandy. In a critical decision, Hitler initially refused to release more than two divisions from Norway when he attacked Russia in June 1941. His depleted force in the north sector failed to cut off Russia's main supply line to the west by not by taking Murmansk, only seventy-four miles away. Had it been successful, this rarely noted operation would have had a disastrous impact on Russia's war effort.

Norway's merchant fleet, third largest but most modern in the world, went over to the Allies virtually intact. More than one thousand ships and 27,500 crewmen headed for British and neutral ports when King Haakon called for Norwegians to resist the Germans. They were crucial in transporting oil and supplies for the Allies during the rest of the war.

Norway's Norsk Hydro plant produced 99 percent of the world's supply of deuterium oxide, or "heavy water." German scientists mistakenly believed that heavy water was the only moderator to control fission for atom bomb research and development. With control of the plant, Germany felt little urgency to develop an atom bomb. The Allies, without heavy water, were forced to consider other possibilities, and Enrico Fermi discovered highly refined graphite to also work as a moderator to control fisson.

Much has been made of the strategic importance of Norway as a northern base for German submarines to attack and seriously hamper Allied convoys to England and Russia. One naval historian has pointed out, however, that without those bases Germany might well have paid more attention to the American coast. There they had an average of only nine subs and a maximum of eighteen, but with the backdrop of lights along the coast from Miami to New York, these sank far more ships per underwater raider and with less risk than submarines in the North Atlantic and around Norway's North Cape.

The German invasion also caused a backlash among Americans of Scandinavian heritage, particularly Norwegians, who were previously inclined to isolationism and non-involvement in the war. Their shift to an anti-Nazi position in the politically important Midwest helped President Roosevelt gather congressional and public support for aid to Britain.

The occupation lasted five years, at great cost to Norway.

- Germans took nearly 40 percent of all goods and services (gross domestic product).
- Half of Norway's shipping fleet was destroyed.
- 10,000 lives were lost including 4,000 seamen.
- 40,000 Norwegians were imprisoned.
- Norway was burdened with nearly 400,000 Germans, highest per capita of any nation.
- By 1945 the average prewar 2,500 calories of food per day was cut in half.

Of the occupied nations, only Denmark suffered less because of its "special accommodation" with Germany. But Norway, through passive resistance and very sophisticated sabotage, was a millstone around Germany's neck.

The unintended consequences and ultimate effect of the invasion of this small nation on the outcome of World War II is amazing and yet virtually unrecognized. A little over a thousand years earlier, the Vikings were center stage in Western civilization. Their descendents were the targets and unwilling witnesses of one of history's other great turning points.

Military and Naval Anecdotes

I n 1935 the Labor Party, which had almost half the seats in the Storting (parliament), took control of the Norwegian government for the first time since Norway gained independence from Sweden in 1905. Although the party was responsible for much of the nation's pioneering social legislation, it had a strong pacifist agenda that severely curtailed defense spending in deference to other needs. Also, compulsory military training was only thirteen weeks long, the least of any European nation. By 1938, however, the storm clouds in Europe and Hitler's arms buildup forced Norway to reconsider its pacifist stance. Initial steps were quite unusual and sometimes comical.

Norway's first attempt to upgrade its small, antiquated air force resulted in a contract with Italy to supply nine Caproni twin-engine combination transport/light bombers. They could also be fitted with skis for winter operation. They were far from suitable, according to experts; Norway's decision was based on Italy's willingness to accept payment in dried codfish, and Norway's fish industry needed help. Initial deliveries were so disappointing that Norway had to come up with hard cash to purchase other aircraft from the United States. Capronis with skis did have some use, however. In the early weeks of the invasion, they were able to take off from a heavily snow-blanketed field after a group of Laplanders (Sami) had their reindeer herd trample down the snow. Payment was several bottles of whisky. Unfortunately, the ground crew was kept awake until the small hours

of the morning by the nonstop *yoiking* of the Sami. Alcohol read-
ily brought forth the monotonous chants that alternated between
shrieks and howls and then moaning to proclaim tales of heroic
ancestral Sami deeds and tribal and family history. Amazingly, after
only an hour's sleep, the Sami emerged at dawn from their tents full
of energy, packed all their belongings, folded their tents, and charged
off with their herd.

Norway's defense budget was so tight that only one tank could
be ordered for the cavalry and payment had to be spread out over
several years. The commanding officer said his troopers would at
least "have a chance to see one in their lifetime." The navy's two largest warships were turn-of-the-century vintage ships that had not left
port since 1918 to conserve fuel. Their admiral referred to them affec-
tionately as his "two old bathtubs." The army's commander, General
Laake, did not even have a staff car and missed most of the invasion's
early action. He reluctantly left his country home for headquarters
when finally convinced by subordinates there really was an invasion
in progress. When he arrived at 10:00 a.m., he found headquarters
empty. It had moved north to follow the government with equipment, maps, vehicles, and even his uniform. Without an automobile,
he tried to catch up on a trolley car, then hitchhiked without luck,
and finally made it on foot to a rail station where he caught a train.
His main qualification for the position was his willingness to drasti-
cally cut the defense budget.

Laake was not alone in being mismatched for his role. Carl Mon-
sen, the Defense Minister, an ardent pacifist, conscientious objector,
and member of the Socialist Party's Anti-Militarist Committee in the
1920s, had once been arrested for pacifist agitation and stirring up
unrest among soldiers. When the invasion occurred Laake and For-

eign Minister Koht, unfamiliar with the mobilization process, agreed to a "partial and secret mobilization," not realizing this meant letters would be mailed requiring people to report in forty-eight hours. Fortunately, in his 8:30 a.m. radio address Koht announced a mobilization and most reservists immediately headed to pre-assigned locations. But a fair number reported for duty days later with letters in their hands and, in two instances, at places where the Germans were already ensconced and relaxing. One minister huffily said, "How should we know? It was our first time!" More concerned with Russian intentions, the government had earlier sent half its 13,000-man army for maneuvers in the farthest north section of the country. The remaining coastal units did not function well in the nighttime confusion and were outwitted by the Germans. But not in all cases: around five o'clock the morning of the invasion, there was "a shot that was not heard round the world but that may have changed the course of history," according to the eminent historian John Lukacs.

The main German flotilla in the invasion headed up the Oslofjord toward the capitol, led by Germany's newest heavy cruiser, *Bluecher*. About two-thirds of the way, it neared a narrow section and the island fort of Oscarsborg. Built by Sweden during the Crimean War almost a hundred years before, the fort mounted three German-made Krupp 1905 Model 11-inch cannons, some smaller artillery pieces, and an adjacent bank of land-based torpedoes. Colonel Birger Eriksen, in command and near retirement, had been strictly ordered not to open fire for any reason until given permission from Oslo. Because of reported gunfire at the fjord entrance, Eriksen was out keeping watch when he saw the silhouette of the *Bluecher* passing in front of lights further down the fjord. When the cruiser came abreast, Eriksen ordered a brilliant search light on the opposite shore switched on. It provided a beautiful target outline of the *Bluecher* with its guns pointing disdainfully dead ahead as it steamed past. Eriksen gave the order to fire one round each from two of the 11-inch guns. He did not think their condition would allow more than a single shot. With amazing luck, one shell struck the *Bluecher's* control tower and another hit ammunition and aviation fuel stored on the afterdeck.

The cruiser began to steer erratically, and the blazing fire on deck made it an even better target for smaller weapons. Then the fort's torpedoes were let go and two slammed into the hull with devastating effect. The sea was an inferno of burning oil as the ship listed and men struggled to reach shore. Eventually it capsized and sank. Nearly a thousand Germans went down with it, along with all the Gestapo records as well as files and administrative personnel for the new government. A pocket battleship, destroyers, and transports in the flotilla turned back and landed troops further down the fjord. Instead of arriving at the Oslo docks around 6:00 a.m. and seizing the capitol, king, and government, German troops with a marching band did not enter the city until noontime and this was from the airport. The king, his ministers, and most of the government had already left Oslo by a special train at 7:30 a.m., followed by a fleet of thirteen trucks loaded with the country's gold reserves. Lukacs again: "Had the king and government been captured in Oslo there would have been no Norwegian campaign, except for Narvik in the far north. The Norwegian campaign brought Churchill to power." And Churchill's leadership was crucial to the Allied victory over Germany.

Few historians know of Colonel Birger Eriksen, a hero who died shortly after the war but not before being decorated by General de

Gaulle of France. It is quite ironic that the three 11-inch guns at Oscarsborg were made in Germany by Krupp, the shore torpedoes that finished off the heavy cruiser were Austrian, and German intelligence had dismissed the fort as little more than a museum with antiquated weapons. It would not be too far-fetched to claim that one Norwegian might have saved civilization.

Around 3:00 a.m., two hours before the invasion officially began, a German secret agent staying at the Victoria Hotel in Stavanger put in a telephone call to his embassy in Oslo. He said he was in contact with the approaching ships offshore and asked for his instructions. The voice at the other end replied in perfect German, "We have no instructions. This is the Swedish embassy." The German slammed down the telephone. The hotel operator had put through his call to the wrong number! The Swedish duty officer immediately called the Norwegian Foreign Office, where everyone had been on alert wondering whether the British or the Germans were invading. This was one of the first official confirmations that it was Germany.

Postwar analysis of Hitler's library and marginal notes shows a strong interest in military history, with special admiration for the British navy and its traditions. In Norway, spectacular additions to British naval lore came from several glorious destroyer actions. On April 8 the HMS *Glowworm,* with only 4.7-inch guns, was badly damaged off the Norwegian coast by opening rounds from the much larger 8-inch-armed German heavy cruiser *Hipper.* Laboring in a sea of thirty-foot waves and gale force winds and unable to outdistance the Germans, *Glowworm* laid a smokescreen as a shield. She then doubled back behind the screen and, at twenty knots, rammed the surprised *Hipper* as it emerged at flank speed from the smoke, thinking the British had turned tail to escape.

Glowworm, with a damaged stuck siren blaring forth, backed off and fired a last salvo before *Hipper,* pounding away at point-blank range, blew up *Glowworm's* magazine. Her captain, Lt. Cmdr. Broadmead-Roope, calmly lighting a cigarette, gave the order to abandon ship as she was going down with virtually all hands. Only one officer and thirty seamen could be rescued by the *Hipper* that stood by in one of the oldest traditions of the sea. Roope fell back while being pulled to safety and drowned. Ironically, for years he had been nicknamed "Rammer Roope." The 150-foot gash on *Hipper's* side impaired her seaworthiness, but of greater importance was the signal from *Glowworm* giving the Admiralty its first indication of the German navy's location and intentions. Germany was not making a break out into the North Sea as Churchill first thought, but was racing up the coast with warships jam-packed with troops, two hundred per destroyer and up to one thousand on pocket battleships. It was a brilliant move.

Just as dramatic, two days later the HMS *Hardy* led five destroyers in the pre-dawn hours through a blinding snowstorm in narrow fjords to Narvik's harbor. With complete surprise, they destroyed most of the newly arrived German ships. Returning, they were spotted by German destroyers they had previously eluded and the *Hardy* was badly shot up. Sinking, her mortally wounded captain had her driven full speed onto the shore to save the crew. This action and a follow-up three days later by Britain's battleship *Warspite* resulted in the destruction of all ten of Germany's most modern destroyers, several supply ships, a tanker, and in spectacular fashion, an ammunition supply ship. Commanders of both the *Glowworm* and the *Hardy* earned posthumous Victoria Crosses, Britain's highest decoration. These naval losses by Germany were to have dire results.

Britain had less success on land. Troops lined up for embarkation wore long, thick fur coats with giant oversized boots and heavy socks. They could hardly move, much less handle weapons. A general observing them said they looked like "paralyzed bears." At the eleventh hour, the War Office sent aides racing around to the tourist offices in London for any brochures or maps they could find about Norway. They were certainly unprepared for the giant snowfall in the Trondheim area that second week in April. A general of small stature who wanted to see for himself why so little progress was being made fell in over his head on a soft patch of snow. Two officers of the Scots Guards pulled him out, sputtering like a wet rooster. His monocle as well as his dignity was lost in the plunge. Supplies that had been hastily unloaded when the German fleet was first sighted leaving the Baltic were haphazardly put back. Transports with artillery found their ammunition was in other ships headed for a different destination. In the landing north of Narvik, desk furniture had to be unloaded first onto small boats before essential equipment could be reached and brought ashore. Although lack of artillery, tanks, and air power were deciding factors in the Allied defeat, these details of poor planning and mishaps contributed greatly to Chamberlain's fall.

Britain's counter-invasion centered on taking the key northern city of Trondheim. Since the Germans enjoyed vast air superiority, the British contacted a French manufacturer about purchasing barrage balloons in the event Britain was successful. (These were large balloons held down by metal cables which were used to deter low-flying aircraft.) What a wonderful coincidence if this French firm was a successor to the maker of a balloon seventy years earlier that had a most unusual journey. Paris had been taken over by the radical Communards in 1870, at the end of the Franco-Prussian war, and was besieged by the German army. One way to get people and messages out was by balloons. They were launched at night or in fog and kept aloft long enough to get far beyond the German lines. One midnight in November, two Frenchmen, quite thin from the food shortages, went up with a bag of mail for the outside world and a crate of homing pigeons for return messages. They were caught in very strong swirling winds and dense clouds. Not sure of their location or direction and fearful of being caught if they landed too soon, they stayed up in the freezing cold and dense clouds until morning before releasing air to descend. Coming down out of a low cloud, they could see nothing but water. They threw out the mail to lose weight and get back up.

Late that afternoon, they descended again. There was nothing but a vast expanse of white. Near ground they jumped out and landed in deep snow, while the balloon took off with the pigeons. They dug themselves out and spent the night in an abandoned hut. The next day they were staggering toward another hut when fearsome looking animal like creatures with thick fur came bounding towards them, uttering strange guttural noises. Mostly from exhaustion but also from fright, the two little Frenchmen collapsed. Some hours later they awoke side by side in warm comfortable beds. Bustling around them were giant women with long blonde braids wearing voluminous blue, white, and red paneled outfits. The Frenchmen had landed in Norway, over eight hundred miles from Paris, and were in a Christiania (now Oslo) hospital. The Norwegian nurses had hastily sewn together their new outfits in French revolutionary colors to express sympathy with the Commune.

One hundred and thirty years later, the Germans landed outside Oslo, and hearing that the king and government had headed north by rail, a paratroop team commandeered cars to give chase. Before long they ran into a roadblock hastily set up by the Norwegian army. Spraying the area with small arms fire, the Germans confidently rushed forth. Their leader was killed and the team was decimated. The road-blocking unit was composed of members of a local rifle club! The surviving Germans hastily fled back to the airport. Two days later, the Luftwaffe tried to kill the king by strafing and bombing the inn where he was staying. Under a hail of bullets, the king and his ministers raced for shelter in a nearby forest. There were no casualties, but two ministers running through a farmyard tripped and fell face down in a pigsty. In the meeting that followed the raid, they sat a bit apart.

Ironically, Germany's invasion of Norway and control of deuterium oxide, or "heavy water," from the Norsk Hydro plant contributed to its lack of urgency in developing an atomic bomb. Two months before the invasion, German representatives approached Norsk Hydro about purchasing heavy water in very large quantities. The Norsk Hydro managers fended them off when they learned from French intelligence that German interest involved a secret weapon. After the invasion German scientists were ecstatic about controlling virtually the entire world's supply and manufacturing capability for what they assumed was the only moderator to control nuclear fission and successfully develop an atom bomb. In theory there were three possible moderators, and it turned out that highly refined graphite worked as well as "heavy-water" and was easier to get. A top German scientist, Bothe, mistakenly ruled out refined carbon, and this gave Germany even more confidence that its monopoly on heavy water put it well ahead of other nations. About the time of the experiment, Bothe sent a letter to a young lady he fell in love with the previous year while traveling to America. In it he said that although he talked about physics all day, he could think only of her! Japan also considered heavy water the key to a bomb effort but decided it was too costly and too difficult to obtain. The Allies, lacking heavy water, were forced to consider other possibilities. America's vast array of scientists, resources, and President Roosevelt's support afforded exploration of different paths, and Enrico Firmi found highly refined graphite worked.

Besides controlling heavy water, Germany arrogantly felt its scientists were superior as well. Reinforcing this was a memorandum to Hitler from his Washington embassy that discussed how unqualified America's scientists were. This report to Hitler and Albert Speer, Minister of Armaments, in early 1942 created an added sense of security. Germany also believed the war would be too short for the three or four years needed to build a bomb. Rockets, tanks, aircraft, and other weapons, which take months rather than years to develop, were a higher priority. Actually, the Germans never came close to making a bomb, but the dramatic Norwegian sabotage of the heavy water plant and its last shipment was not without justification.

A small group of Norwegians parachuted in from Britain and with the help of the local resistance were able to dynamite the heavy water plant and stop production for months. Then innumerable Allied air raids failed to do any damage, but Germany decided the operation was too vulnerable to remain in Norway. When the machinery and last supplies were being shipped by rail to the Baltic, three members of the Norwegian resistance hid explosives in the bilge of a ferry with a timer set to go off as it crossed a long, deep lake. It worked beautifully, and the ferry sunk in water too deep for recovery. This was not only reported to be the most heavily guarded German shipment in the war but General George Marshall, the U.S. Army chief of staff, had ordered all the U.S. air forces in Britain to stop the shipment "at any cost" if it reached the Baltic Sea. The Allies feared that radioactive dust from a nuclear pile using heavy water could be spread over England with lethal long-range effects. After the 1931 discovery of this heavy hydrogen isotope in a California laboratory, experiments were conducted to see if it had beneficial properties for plants and animals. Tests on a mouse using the last batch showed no discernable effects other than "marked signs of intoxication."

Bibliography and Suggested Reading

Adamson, Hans Christian and Per Klem. *Blood On the Midnight Sun.* W.W. Norton, New York, 1965.

Astrup, Helen and B.L. Jacot. *Night Has a Thousand Eyes: An Account of a Resistance Worker in Norway.* Macdonald & Co., London, 1953.

Broch, Theodor. *The Mountains Wait.* Webb Book Publishing Co., St. Paul, Minn., 1942.

Claasen, Adam R.A. *Hitler's Northern War: The Luftwaffe's Ill-Fated Campaign, 1940-1945.* University Press of Kansas, Lawrence, Kansas, 2001.

Colville, John. *The Fringes of Power, 10 Downing Street Diaries 1939-1955.* W. W. Norton & Company, New York, 1986.

Dagre, Tor. *Norway and World War II.* Norwegian Ministry of Foreign Affairs, Oslo.

Dahl, Per F. *Heavy Water and the Wartime Race for Nuclear Energy.* Institute of Physics Publishing, Bristol and Philadelphia, 1999.

Devins, Joseph H., Jr. *The Vaagso Raid.* Chilton Book Company, Philadelphia, 1967.

Fjellbu, Arne. *Memoirs from the War Years.* Augsburg Publishing, Minneapolis, 1947.

Hambro, C.J. *I Saw It Happen In Norway.* D. Appleton-Century Co., New York, 1940.

Harriman, Florence. *Mission To the North.* J.B. Lippincott Co., Philadelphia, 1941.

Harvey, Maurice. *Scandinavian Misadventure: The Campaign in Norway, 1940.* Spellmount Limited, Tunbridge Wells, Kent, 1990

Haukelid, Knut. *Skis Against the Atom.* William Kimber, London, 1954.

Helmersen, Hanna Aasuik. *War and Innocence.* Hara Publishing, Seattle, 2000.

Howarth, David. *The Shetland Bus.* Thomas Nelson, London, 1951.

Howarth, David. *We Die Alone.* The Macmillan Company, New York, 1955.

Jenkins, Roy. *Churchill, A Biography.* Farrar, Straus and Giroux, New York, 2001.

Jones, Gwyn. *The Vikings.* The Folio Society, London, 1997.

Kersaudy, Francois. *Norway 1940.* University of Nebraska Press, Lincoln, 1987.

Koht, Halvdan and Sigmund Skard. *The Voice of Norway.* Columbia University Press, New York, 1944.

Koht, Halvdan. *Norway, Neutral and Invaded.* The Macmillan Company, New York, 1941.

Liddell Hart, B.H. *History of the Second World War.* G.P. Putnam's Sons, New York, 1971.

Lukacs, John. *Five Days in London, May 1940.* Yale University Press, New Haven, 2001.

Lukacs, John. *The Duel, 10 May-31 July 1940: The Eighty Day Struggle Between Churchill and Hitler.* Ticknor & Fields, New York, 2001.

Mann, Chris and Christer Jorgensen. *Hitler's Arctic War.* Brown Partworks, London, 2003.

Munthe, Malcom. *Sweet Is War.* Gerald Duckworth & Co., Ltd., London, 1954.

Nakiel & Preston. *Atlas of Maritime History.* Gallery Books, New York.

Nansen, Odd. *From Day to Day.* G.P. Putnam's Sons, New York, 1949.

The New Columbia Encyclopedia. Columbia University Press, New York.

Petrow, Richard. *The Bitter Years: The Invasion and Occupation of Denmark and Norway, April 1940-May 1945.* Morrow Quill Paperbacks, Inc., N.Y., 1974.

Read, Anthony Read and David Fisher. *The Deadly Embrace: Hitler, Stalin and the Nazi-Soviet Pact, 1939-1941.* W.W. Norton & Company, New York, 1988.

Rhodes, Richard. *The Making of the Atomic Bomb.* Simon & Schuster, New York, 1995.

Seth, Ronald. *The Noble Saboteurs.* Hawthorn Books, Inc., New York, 1966.

Shirer, William L. *The Rise and Fall of the Third Reich.* Simon & Schuster, New York, 1959.

Stokker, Kathleen. *Folklore Fights the Nazis.* University of Wisconsin Press, 1997.

Storhaug, Hans. *Hotell i saerklasse, Victoria Hotel, Stavanger 1900-2000.* Billedredaktor Halvor Pedersen.

Strawson, John. *Churchill and Hitler.* Fromm International, New York, 1997.

Stuart, Lyle. *Report From No. 24.* Gunnar Sonsteby, New York, 1965.

Wright, Myrtle. *Norwegian Diary, 1940-1945.* Friends Peace International Relations, 1974.